# Low-Maintenance Vegetable Gardening

## Bumper Crops in Minutes a Day Using Raised Beds, Planning, and Plant Selection

Clare Matthews

COMPANIONHOUSE
B O O K S

*Low-Maintenance Vegetable Gardening*

CompanionHouse Books™ is an imprint of Fox Chapel Publishers International Ltd.

Project Team
Vice President–Content: Christopher Reggio
Editor: Anthony Regolino
Copy Editor: Kaitlyn Ocasio
Design: Mary Ann Kahn and Justin Speers
Index: Elizabeth Walker

ISBN 978-1-62008-247-8
The Cataloging-in-Publication Data is on file with the Library of Congress.

This book has been published with the intent to provide accurate and authoritative information in regard to the subject matter within. While every precaution has been taken in the preparation of this book, the author and publisher expressly disclaim any responsibility for any errors, omissions, or adverse effects arising from the use or application of the information contained herein.

Fox Chapel Publishing
903 Square Street
Mount Joy, PA 17552

Fox Chapel Publishers International Ltd.
7 Danefield Road, Selsey (Chichester)
West Sussex PO20 9DA, U.K.

www.facebook.com/companionhousebooks

We are always looking for talented authors. To submit an idea, please send a brief inquiry to acquisitions@foxchapelpublishing.com.

Printed and bound in Singapore
20 19 18    2 4 6 8 10 9 7 5 3 1

# CONTENTS

# Introduction

Growing your own fruit and vegetables has so many advantages. Nothing beats the taste of produce homegrown for flavor rather than for how well it travels or for uniform size and shape. Then, of course, there is the excitement and magic of watching your produce grow and the delight of the first harvest. Finally, let's not forget the superior levels of nutrients in freshly picked vegetables and the chance to work with nature in a fast-moving world where a connection to the land can seem ever more remote.

# Introduction

At a time when we are becoming far more aware of the importance of the quality of what we eat and the impact food production has on the environment, growing your own is incredibly popular. However, there are still those who are put off by a lack of knowledge and time. But for previous generations, growing your own was second nature.

I remember, as a child, following my grandfather around his pristine, traditional vegetable garden as he gathered a basketful of faultless produce for my family to take home. As we worked our way around the magical plot, I would nibble on tender peas straight from the plant and strawberries warm from the sun. For him, growing great vegetables was just a part of life. As an enthusiastic gardener I always wanted to give my family the same fantastic experience, and while I'd previously dabbled, it wasn't until a few years ago that my family bought a rural retreat and I had the chance to build a real vegetable patch.

There was, however, a major drawback: for the most part, I would only be able to tend my vegetable patch on weekends, and even then there would be plenty of other demands on my time, such as my work and, as a mother with three children, a chaotic family life. Hiring help wasn't an option because I actually enjoyed the business of gardening, working with the seasons and having time to connect with nature and wonder at its marvels. For me, tending the vegetables myself is all part of the pleasure. I discovered that with a few tricks up my sleeve I could spend very little time in the garden for most of the year and still get a good yield. After several years of amazing productivity my weekend vegetable garden has proved to be more successful than even I could have hoped.

In this book I explain the strategies that have made my weekend vegetable patch a success despite my limited and fragmented time for gardening. A mixture of common sense, time-saving techniques, and knowing what is really important makes growing vegetables easy. I confess that at times my vegetables have been beleaguered by weeds and subject to mild and sporadic neglect, but harvests have always been good and phenomenally tasty. True, more care may have given me marginally better yields, but I still produce more than enough to make the whole project worthwhile.

So read on and follow my advice for achieving a successful and beautiful low-maintenance vegetable garden. Good luck, but most of all, enjoy!

— **Clare Matthews**

▶ A small sample of the myriad of marvelous tastes, colors, and textures you can look forward to from your vegetable plot.

# The Keys to Success

Once you have decided to embark on a grow-your-own project, the first step is to plan a layout for your vegetable plot that is practical, easy to manage, and not too ambitious. The way your vegetable plot is laid out, its size and the arrangement of the beds, the construction of the paths, and even the location of the garden will go a long way toward determining how easy it is to maintain and how productive it will be.

## Plan Ahead

- Decide what you want to grow at the beginning of the year, make a "to grow" list, and stick to it. Place an order with a nursery for delivery in late winter so that your seeds, plants, tubers, and sets arrive at just the right time for planting, relieving you of a great deal of planning and thinking.
- Carefully consider how many plants you need to grow to feed your family and plan exactly where to plant them. Giving away tasty homegrown vegetables feels great, but an extreme glut of one crop is a waste of time and growing space. Leafing through nursery catalogs is tremendously inspiring but there is no point in ordering plants you don't have the space to grow. The listings on pages 48–161 give a very rough indication of how much of each crop it is reasonable to grow, but this is only a starting point. Experience will show what works for you.
- Use a notebook to keep lists, information on successes and failures, and repeat sowing plans handy. This doesn't have to be anything fancy, just practical, as it will inevitably end up a bit grubby.

## Keep It Simple

- Grow a high proportion of undemanding crops that deliver a prodigious harvest for the minimum of work, especially if you are a beginner. These generous, forgiving plants are the mainstays of the low-maintenance vegetable plot. Avoid the unreliable, demanding prima donnas of the vegetable world. Information on the easy-going plants and their fussier fellows are on pages 44–47. Just because a plant is undemanding doesn't make it less worth growing—potatoes are one of the least fussy there is, but nothing compares to the taste of freshly dug potatoes.
- Choose varieties with disease and pest resistance wherever possible. This gives an obvious head start in protecting precious crops. The plant listings on pages 48–161 suggest some disease-resistant varieties, but since this is such an advantage, plant breeders are developing new cultivars all the time.

▶ Both the leek 'Pancho' and beets (beetroot) 'Boltardy' are reliable, useful cultivars that taste great.

- Grow most crops from transplant (plug plants), or young plants ready to go straight into the garden. This will save a great deal of time, although initially it may feel like a bit of a cheat as we tend to think that real gardeners labor over seed trays, wrestle with the problems of germination and damping off, spend hours pricking out, and worry about keeping the greenhouse at the right temperature. However, if, like me, you just don't have time for all this, leave it to the experts and order healthy young plants to arrive at your door at just the right time for planting. It is more expensive than growing everything from seed, but I don't run a greenhouse and my homegrown vegetables are still much less expensive and tastier than those sold in stores. I also get exactly the number of plants I need, making harvests more predictable.
- Only grow from seed when it can be sown directly into the ground and won't require a great deal of pampering.
- Use the organic "no-dig" system described on page 166 to manage the soil. This means that the traditional, physically demanding tilling (digging over) of the plot each autumn becomes unnecessary. Instead, a mulch of compost (garden compost) or well-rotted farmyard manure is spread on the soil early in the year and the worms are left to do the rest, dragging the organic matter down into the soil. Applying mulch is easier than digging, and what's even better is that this shortcut uses natural processes to improve fertility and is actually better for the soil than all that time-consuming hard labor.
- Use a variety of mulches to reduce weeds and the need to water. Many materials suitable for use as mulches are quick and easy to spread and freely available. Applying mulch suppresses weed growth, reduces moisture loss from the soil, and is much easier than weeding. See pages 168–169 for information on marvelous, time-saving mulches.
- Install a simple irrigation system and water wisely. Watering is a chore that seems to overwhelm many vegetable growers, quite unnecessarily, and people are inclined to water too much or in the wrong way. I am positively miserly with water, encouraging plants to put down good roots and so become much less susceptible to drought. There are many plants that will not need watering most of the time, but there are times when you have to water, for example when plants are getting established, and on other occasions when a few gallons of water will really boost yield. The most basic of irrigation systems can take care of the work and the worry of watering. Components can be bought at most DIY stores and are easier to put together than most children's construction sets. If you leave the garden to fend for itself for long periods, then an adjustable irrigation system is essential. See pages 36–37 for more on this.
- Don't run a greenhouse. The maintenance takes time, keeping the ventilation and temperature just right is an exacting task, and purchasing and running a greenhouse can be costly. By buying crops as small plants or sowing seed directly into the soil, the need for a greenhouse is avoided and things are kept simple.
- Take steps to prevent problems with pests and diseases. This is a much easier strategy than trying to eradicate a pest or disease once it has a good foothold, especially if, like me, you have decided to do without chemical quick fixes. If you only visit your plot on the weekend or once or twice a week, plenty of damage can be done before you know it, robbing you of your eagerly awaited harvest.
- Talk to local experienced gardeners. Ask them about the soil, what grows well, and which pests are a problem. This is a much quicker route to accumulating knowledge than spending years gardening on a trial-and-error basis. Most gardeners are only too happy to share their tips and triumphs and bemoan their failures.

Perfect for Halloween, these 'Racer' pumpkins are remarkably simple to grow and a great first plant for children. However, they occupy a good deal of growing area and may not be a sensible use of space in a small plot.

## Work on the Soil

- Good, fertile soil gives you the best chance of growing trouble-free fruit and vegetables. There is little point in launching enthusiastically into the planting and sowing of seeds until your soil is somewhere near right. It is the one area where you just can't cut corners. Put simply, the soil nourishes the plants that will hopefully nourish you, and a fertile, living soil is more likely to produce the bumper crops we all want.
- Plants in fertile soil will be stronger and better able to withstand hardship. The "no-dig" system described on page 166 delivers a fertile soil naturally.

## Adopt a Relaxed Approach

- Know which tasks take priority and focus on them in the time you have. If you are short on time the secret to gardening well is knowing how best to spend what little you have. Getting seeds and plants into the ground is always the most urgent task (if this doesn't get done there will be no vegetables), along with checking on what needs watering or adjusting the irrigation system. Anything else can wait if it has to.
- Turn a blind eye to innocuous weeds in unimportant places until you have time to deal with them. Some weeds really can be left, without guilt, for a while. Others are best tackled quickly to save time and trouble later. The details of this pragmatic approach to weeding are explained on page 179.
- Expect a few failures. All gardeners have them, and sometimes they are completely inexplicable.
- If you are producing tasty fruit and vegetables you have succeeded, even if your plot is not glossy-magazine perfection. Have realistic expectations; with buckets of time, money, and staff anyone could run a perfect-looking plot, with row upon row of vegetables of every description and the soil looking good enough to eat. Most of us, however, have to settle for something a little less than perfect, but that can still be brilliantly productive.

## Make It Enjoyable

- Grow produce you really want to eat. Keeping the initial bout of enthusiasm going is vital—if your vegetable plot project is to work it needs to have tangible rewards, so growing things you can't wait to eat is important. Why waste time and space growing cabbage if you rarely eat it when you could be growing something you find delicious?
- Begin with just a few crops to avoid the vegetable garden becoming a burden. Keeping everything on a manageable scale ensures that your grow-your-own project remains a pleasure and not a chore. As soon as it begins to feel like a weighty responsibility, the pleasure evaporates, leading to neglect and failure. Start small, gain skills and confidence, and then take on more. This is particularly relevant if time is in short supply.
- Make your plot a great place to spend time and have some fun. If time in the garden is precious, it is much nicer to spend that time in a pretty, charming, comfortable space, even if you are working. Include decorative set pieces and benches or chairs for a quick cup of tea or coffee. Use companion planting and flowers for cutting to infuse the productive rows with color and scent and your vegetable patch will soon become a wonderful place to spend time. Pages 214–217 explain how to make your kitchen garden special.

Having a few basic tools in a handy trug or basket that can be grabbed en route to the vegetable patch is a real time-saver.

# PART I
# Design, Construction, and Planning

If you want everything in your vegetable plot to run smoothly and without unnecessary effort, getting things right at the planning stage really helps. A bit of thought, research, and time spent considering the space available will ensure that you get your garden off to the best possible start. Moreover, with easily maintained beds, practical paths, and a "to grow" list, the garden will keep the family savoring nutritious, homegrown produce throughout the year. Building your garden will be the most costly and time-consuming part of your grow-your-own endeavor, but you don't necessarily need DIY skills or an enormous budget. There are myriad ways to build a garden, from a simple bed dug in an area of grass to an intricate, geometric pattern of brick-edged raised beds.

# Design

## Choosing the Right Location

Choosing the right location is the best way to start if you want to grow great vegetables with the minimum of effort. Give the vegetable plot the best growing space in the garden and you will be saving yourself the struggle of trying to modify an area that is less than perfect. While it is perfectly possible to improve the negative aspects of some sites, it is just easier not to. The ideal location is fairly sunny and sheltered with good, well-drained soil that is not prone to flooding, becoming waterlogged, or drying out completely, and where there is no competition from the roots of large trees or areas of shade.

Some difficulties can be overcome. A windy site, for instance, can be protected by adding a windbreak in the form of fencing or a trellis or wires held on posts that are used to support rugged climbers. Poor soil can be worked on and beefed up or escaped by building raised beds (see pages 17–18) and a shady area might be opened up by careful pruning. If the plot has to be close to the house, it can be prettied up enough to be proud of. But regardless of the situation, be realistic about what you can achieve.

**THE BASICS**

Give your vegetable plot the area with the most favorable growing conditions in the garden. The ideal is a fairly sunny, sheltered spot, with good soil and good drainage.

## Size

Having a large, beautiful, and bountiful kitchen garden is a wonderful dream, but it pays not to get too adventurous too soon, especially if you are a first-time gardener. Getting behind with the work on the vegetable plot or having too many problems with pests and diseases to deal with can soon lead to poor yields and, worse, disillusionment. It is much better to have a patch half or a quarter of the size of the dream garden in your imagination, enabling you to enjoy the time you spend in the garden and gather a healthy harvest. The project is then a pleasure and a triumph rather than a burden, and you can always expand your plot as your knowledge and confidence grows.

My vegetable plot, for example, has been extended twice and is now four times its original area. It started from very tentative beginnings with just ten small, pretty raised beds covering an area of 182 square feet (17 square meters) with the addition of four much larger growing areas during the second year. This all went well, so I added another four large beds in the third year, giving me a total growing area of just over 720 square feet (67 square meters). The final addition was a modest asparagus bed, and while I would dearly love more space, this is the maximum area I'm comfortable managing, and I know not to be too ambitious.

If you have a community garden plot and the space is too daunting to begin with, try sharing with friends or offering a section to a fellow community gardener whose plot is bursting at the seams. Or it is perfectly acceptable to allow half to lie fallow for a while under a mulch of heavy black plastic or green manure until you are ready to expand.

**THE BASICS**

Start small, gain confidence and skills, then expand your plot.

# Raised Beds

Growing in beds, raised or otherwise, is an alternative to the open or community garden-style productive garden. It is very efficient and offers plenty of benefits for those trying to cut down on the time spent maintaining their vegetable garden. I really don't think I could successfully manage my plot any other way. It reduces an overwhelming expanse of land into easily tackled chunks, saving time and effort.

A raised bed is a planting area with a soil level significantly above the natural soil level, normally contained within a frame and surrounded by permanent paths. Although often constructed from wood, raised beds can be made from just about anything durable that will form a frame to hold soil. Brick, stone, or low hurdles all work well, although hurdles are not particularly robust or long-lived. The simplest raised bed is constructed of lumber—reclaimed scaffolding boards are perfect—which are nailed or screwed to stakes hammered into the ground. My first set of raised beds was made by a local carpenter out of very chunky lumber with lovely mortise and tenon joints at each corner. They are effectively freestanding "flat pack" beds that can be taken apart and rearranged or reused elsewhere. A product of my doubts about how successful my weekend vegetable plot would be, the design gave me the option of transforming the beds into something else, somewhere else, should my doubts have proved right.

## THE BASICS

Raised above the normal soil level and constructed of wood, brick, or other durable materials, raised beds allow you to create excellent, fertile soil and escape problems with bad drainage or thin soil. Crops can be grown more intensively in raised beds, giving you a better harvest for less effort.

▲ These chunky lumber beds look fantastic, are incredibly practical, and will last for years.

◄ Chic metal raised beds give the vegetable plot a contemporary feel.

This large, ornamental vegetable garden has an arrangement of low beds. Bay trees and teepees add height.

## Advantages of Raised Beds

- Perhaps the most important advantage of all is that raised beds allow you to escape unfavorable soil. This enables you to ensure the best growing conditions possible by filling your beds with a 50-50 mix of good-quality topsoil and well-rotted organic matter to produce great soil and, in turn, vigorous, productive plants. Where the underlying soil is very wet, the ground below the bed needs to be tilled and some gravel or sand worked in before the new soil is added to ensure good drainage. In most circumstances the beds need only be about 12 in. (30 cm) deep, though in very damp areas the depth can be 24 in. (60 cm) or more to ensure good drainage. Higher beds are also an excellent option for gardeners with back problems.

- When growing in raised beds you only need to maintain, water, weed, and cultivate the core growing area. The beds can be planted more intensively by arranging plants with less space between them than in the traditional open vegetable garden or community garden plot, so you get more tasty produce for the area maintained. Closer spacing also cuts down on weeding, too, since more of the soil is covered with plants and the weeds are deprived of light.

- The soil in raised beds warms up more quickly in the spring than soil in an open vegetable garden or community garden plot, allowing plants and seeds to get a faster start.

- Having neat islands of raised garden surrounded by paths makes working in the garden convenient and allows you to harvest crops in all kinds of weather since there is no need to walk on the soil. This is very handy when you are short of time and can't be picky about when you venture outdoors. Growing in beds also works very well with the time-saving "no-dig" method described on page 166.

- Plants are easily protected from frost or pests in a neat, regular, confined area. Wire or plastic pipe hoops that neatly span the bed can hold row covers, chicken wire, or insect-proof mesh.

- A crisp pattern of well-constructed beds will give you a head start in keeping the garden looking neat and well tended. A pretty arrangement of beds instantly makes the garden look more appealing and decorative, adding value and elevating the humble vegetable patch to "truly beautiful kitchen garden." Taking the time to give your plot what is often termed "good bones," being a strong, structured design, will go a long way toward engendering the illusion of tidiness even through those inevitable times of slight neglect.

- If you are lucky enough to have great soil, raised beds may seem unnecessary. In this case, laying out a series of low beds at the existing soil level bounded by permanent paths will give many of the same advantages and can be managed in the same "no-dig" way.

# Layout

The way you choose to lay out your beds will have a big impact on how simple they are to tend and how the garden looks. The neatness and beauty of your plot may not trouble you as you may be in it only for the delicious food, but for most gardeners creating a wonderful space and an area to be proud of helps make tending the garden more of a pleasure and less of a chore.

## How Much Growing Area?

This will be governed by how much space you have available, what kind of crops you hope to grow, and how much you want to take on in the first year. If you aim to concentrate on salad greens, tomatoes, and cucumbers you will only need a few small beds, perhaps measuring 3 x 4 ft. (1 x 1.2 m). If you want to grow bulk crops like onions and potatoes then more cultivated space and larger beds will be more practical, perhaps 10–16 x 4 ft. (3–5 x 1.2 m). A combination of large and small beds will suit most people and will make for interesting design possibilities. I started with 182 square feet (17 square meters) and this was easily manageable, but this setup lacked the longer beds ideal for bulk crops.

## What Size and Shape Beds?

The basic rule is that a bed can be as long as you like but only ever less than twice your arm's length wide, meaning that you can tend the bed, weed, harvest, and mulch without ever having to walk on the soil. However, in reality very long beds can become a nuisance as you move around the garden. Square and rectangular beds are easiest to cultivate; while intricate shapes, triangles, and circles may look fantastic, they are hard to construct and tend. It is well worth carefully measuring your area and drawing out your proposed pattern to scale, leaving space for decorative elements like benches, trees, or whatever takes your fancy. There is nothing wrong with taking the easy option either; if you plan to use scaffolding boards, making beds the length of each board or half a board cuts down work and is economical. If you have old paving stones to use for paths, make the length of your beds fit neatly with these to avoid cutting stones or having oddly constructed paths and corners.

## THE BASICS

Beds should be narrow enough to be tended without stepping on the soil, ideally between 3 ft. (1 m) and 4 ft. (1.2 m) wide, and as long as is practical. Complex-shaped beds are likely to be less convenient.

An intricate pattern of box-edged beds makes this vegetable plot very attractive, although maybe not the easiest to maintain.

# Paths

There is nothing more irritating than trying to maneuver a fully loaded wheelbarrow around tight corners or in confined spaces. So at least some of your paths need to be wide enough to turn a wheelbarrow, keeping in mind that if all has gone to plan by mid summer the beds will be literally overflowing with an abundance of vegetables. To save space, secondary paths can be just wide enough to walk along, so long as all beds are accessible from the major pathways.

The surface of the path is also important. If you are converting a patch of lawn to a productive garden, then the temptation might be to keep the areas of grass between beds as the paths—this is cheap and easy, and I have to concede that carefully mown, lush green grass paths look fabulous. However, mowing the paths takes time, trimming or clipping up against beds is fiddly, and lush green paths soon become slippery or threadbare when the weather is very wet or hot. All-weather surfaces are much more practical; gravel, brick, or concrete slabs work well. For ease, economy, good looks, and practicality, gravel wins for me. It never gets slippery, drains easily, and constructing a gravel path can be done quickly by almost anyone. Any weeds are a cinch to remove as there is little to get their roots into.

## Building a Gravel Path

To lay a gravel path in a vegetable garden it is sufficient to cover the area of the path with a heavy-duty weed-suppressing landscape fabric. If possible, tuck the edges of the fabric under the sides of the beds to keep weeds from finding even the hint of a chink of light. Pin down the fabric with large-headed plastic landscape fabric pins and allow a generous overlap where edges meet, then add a 2–3 in. (5–7.5 cm) layer of gravel. Any more and walking becomes hard work; any less and bald patches constantly appear. The same method could be used to build a bark chip path, but this is not nearly so practical or attractive. Bark chips tend to hold moisture, clogging together in wet weather, sticking to boots and barrow, and eventually they will break down and need regular replenishing.

## THE BASICS

Main paths should be wide enough for a wheelbarrow to turn, even when the beds are overflowing with luscious vegetables.

Use a rugged, all-weather surface.

◄ A decorative brick path is a practical and attractive option in the vegetable garden.

▶ This beautiful path of brick diamonds infilled with gravel is lavish in width and construction, in keeping with this rather grand vegetable garden.

# Designing the Beds

Ignoring practical considerations will result in a garden that is not as straightforward to look after as it could be. However, practical and delightful can go hand in hand. If you are concerned only with the practical, you have less to think about in laying out your garden, but also much less to look forward to!

A simple geometric pattern of beds works well in both respects. This approach naturally creates vistas and spaces for focal points—this might be a simple bench or standard bay, a rustic scarecrow, or even a piece of sculpture. It is your garden—you can make it as decorative as you want and in your own style, for you to enjoy. Ballerina fruit trees, teepees, standard bays, and trellises can all be used to add some height. (This aspect of the vegetable garden is dealt with on pages 214–217.) As you draw out the pattern of your beds, don't forget to leave space for some decorative and fun elements if it appeals to you.

One word of caution—the kitchen garden tradition, seen perhaps at its most grand in the chateaux of France, often employs a multitude of small box-edged beds, or those edged with lavender. This looks fantastic but really cuts down on the growing space in each bed, and larger beds are required for bulk crops such as potatoes. It can be frustrating to see a large part of the growing area you have worked hard to create supporting an unproductive plant and suffer the inconvenience of working over the low hedge.

If you start small, your successes will undoubtedly inspire you to extend your vegetable patch. It is worth considering how you might do this when planning phase one, leaving options for the further seamless development of the plot. After a couple of seasons growing, you will have a better idea of what works for you and your family.

The best temporary garden seating is the traditional deck chair—perfect for relaxing in after a burst of gardening.

## THE BASICS

A strong, geometric pattern of beds looks good.

Include decorative elements that appeal to you.

My vegetable garden in its first year during early summer. It soon became a favorite place to relax in and watch the vegetables grow.

# Construction

## Preparing the Ground

It would be a rare and fine thing if you were fortunate enough to be starting your vegetable garden in an area of perfect, cultivated soil; it is probably at best turf or more likely a neglected mixture of weeds and brambles. There are a number of ways these might be dealt with, some much less work than others. It is worth remembering that getting the preparation right and making the soil as weed free as possible at this stage is in fact a time-saving strategy—dealing with weeds in an empty plot is much simpler than when they pop up among a row of onions or carrot seedlings.

### Clearing the Ground by Digging

There is no way to dress it up—clearing the ground by digging is backbreaking, time-consuming, hard work where attention to detail is paramount. If you are a time-poor gardener this may not appeal to you, although I have heard of those who have tried to evoke a party spirit to make the task more bearable, inviting friends along to help, with the promise of good food and wine later! Great, so long as the quality of work stays high. Essentially, this is weeding on a grand scale, and as such the golden rule of weeding applies—"get the entire root out." The longer the space has been neglected the tougher the job will be, as some perennial plants have roots that spread great distances and to amazing depths. Any short section of root or rhizome left in the ground will grow into a new plant. The reality is that it is impossible to successfully remove all the roots and this is but the first strike in an ongoing battle, so it pays to make this clearance as effective as possible to make regrowth weak and easy to manage. If you are anxious for a quick fix don't be tempted to try a rototiller—this will just cut weed roots into tiny pieces and replant them all over the area, spreading the problem and ensuring weeds will persist for years to come.

### Clearing the Ground by Covering

This is really only an option if you are not in a hurry to get growing. Rather than removing the weeds, they are killed by depriving them of light by first trimming or stamping down the top growth and then covering the whole area with thick cardboard, thick black plastic, or heavy-duty weed-suppressing landscape fabric.

This must be held down securely and in a way that you are happy to look at for some time as it could take up to three seasons for the toughest of weeds to die. You could compromise and clear half your plot the hard way by digging and cover the remaining part of the garden for a couple of seasons and then perhaps grow potatoes in the covered area. Growing potatoes on newly cultivated ground has the advantage of keeping weed regrowth down, since soil is moved around as they are earthed up. Alternatively, growing potatoes through a sheet mulch of black plastic also suppresses weeds.

### Clearing the Ground by Spraying

Using a chemical spray to clear the ground takes maybe the least effort, although it is not as straightforward as you may think. The results are not instant, plants may take several weeks to die, and established weeds will probably regrow and require a further treatment. So the whole process may take a couple of months. There are several suitable chemicals on the market, but read the manufacturer's instructions carefully and choose one fit for the purpose, rather than one that persists in the soil. If, like me, you'd prefer to run your vegetable patch without resorting to herbicides and pesticides, this isn't an option. It's a personal choice, but I choose to grow as organically as I can, since I will be feeding the food I grow to my family and friends.

### Preparing the Ground by Deep-Layer Mulching

As an incredibly time-efficient way to clear a new area of ground and simultaneously create a fertile growing medium, deep-layer mulching (or lasagna gardening) will appeal to those who like a good shortcut. This method of establishing a new growing area is not without work, but it is less tedious and requires no weeding, plus you create a great growing medium in the process. I have used this method to both clear ground and rescue beds that have been neglected, and it has worked well.

Basically, the turf or weeds are buried under a layer of either corrugated cardboard or a thick wad of newspaper, followed by layers of organic matter, and finally compost or topsoil. Buried under the thick layers and deprived of light, the weeds should die and the paper layer will gradually rot away. Annual weeds do not survive being deeply buried. In theory some perennials might, but in my experience few do and those that do reappear are weak and easy to deal with.

Deep-layer mulching can be done within the raised bed frame or in low beds, where it will raise the soil level into a nice, free-draining hump. There is a whole range of organic material that can be used to build up the layers, but if you have anything you suspect may contain weed seeds it should be put under the cardboard or paper weed barrier. The trick is to add the material in layers—lush green material should be followed by a coarser material like old plant stems or straw so that decomposition happens quickly and effectively. Use layers of about 6 in. (15 cm) thick or less, build up a minimum of 10–12 in. (25–30 cm), and finish with a layer of homemade compost or topsoil. You could build mulch deeper than this if you have the material available or if you add to the bed over time, starting in the autumn for planting in the spring, say. As the material rots to produce a fantastically fertile growing material the level will drop. Accumulating the material may take a bit of planning, but fortunately almost everything you need should be available for free. Stables are normally only too pleased to part with manure, grass clippings can be begged from neighbors, and coarse garden and kitchen waste stockpiled. You can do this over a number of weeks so long as you get enough material down to begin with to check the weeds. In the first year the resulting soil may be a little rough, depending on how you have built your layers.

## Suitable Materials for Deep-Layer Mulching

- Well-rotted manure
- Hay (below the weed barrier)
- Straw
- Plant-based kitchen waste
- Leaf mold
- Leaves (use in thin layers or mixed with something else as they tend to clump together in a mat)
- Grass clippings
- Wood ash
- Seaweed
- Plant debris
- Newspaper
- Compost

▶ Transformed from rough ground to fertile bed by deep-layer mulching, in an hour or so the area is ready for planting.

# THE BASICS

Time consuming, removing all top growth and roots by hand.

Rototilling can increase a weed problem.

Killing all plant life by excluding light with a covering for at least a year.

Using chemicals to kill all plant life.

Covering the area to be cleared with paper or cardboard and a thick layer of organic matter produces a very fertile soil.

# Creating a Deep-Layer Mulch Bed

1. Trim or stamp down the vegetation growing on the area to be cultivated and remove any large pieces of debris or stones. Water the ground thoroughly if it is dry. Lay down the cardboard or newspaper several sheets thick, covering the whole area and leaving a generous overlap of at least 6 in. (15 cm) where pieces meet.

2. Start adding layers of organic material, each about 2–3 in. (5–7 cm) thick. Alternate lush green material, such as grass clippings, with coarser material like straw or old plant stems, including layers of compost if you have it.

3. Add a final thick layer of compost or topsoil. If you are planting small seeds in your bed, then the final layer will need to be a fine (and probably store-bought) planting mix.

4. The deep-layer mulch bed is now ready. Beans, potatoes, zucchinis (courgettes), summer squash (marrows), winter squash, and perennials such as rhubarb will thrive in their first year in the rich mix you have created.

# First Phase of My Vegetable Patch

A fair bit of time and expense went into the construction of my first small vegetable garden, although subsequent phases were much less lavish. However, such time and expense are not essential, and the general principles I employed will apply to many vegetable gardens. I started with an undulating area of rough grass peppered with weeds such as dock, creeping buttercup, and dandelions. I decided to have this leveled to make matters simpler. If you embark upon any leveling activity, be sure to preserve as much topsoil as you can and return it to the site over the subsoil once it is level. Also avoid creating what is known as a pan, where the soil becomes compacted and then drains badly.

I share my rural garden area with rabbits, deer, and badgers, so to avoid also sharing my vegetables I surrounded the plot with 6 ½ ft. (2 m) high wildlife-proof fencing. The beds are made from 8 ¾ x 2 in. (22 x 5 cm) lumber with mortise and tenon joints at the corners. I had the wooden beds put together by a local carpenter, and I designed them to be freestanding and essentially "flatpack" so once they were hammered together on-site I could shuffle them around to get the best layout possible.

Very heavy-duty weed-suppressing landscape fabric was used to cover the areas of the paths and tucked firmly under the edges of the beds and pinned down with a good overlap. It really is worthwhile making sure the weeds have no way through.

A weed-suppressing landscape fabric covers the soil and was cut from the insides of the beds where necessary, leaving a generous margin to prevent weeds from finding a way through.

◄ The corners of the beds are held in place with mortise and tenon joints cut by a carpenter.

▲ Gravel paths leave plenty of space to maneuver wheelbarrows around the garden. The simple layout looks neat and tidy.

# Making Rope Supports

Vegetable gardens can be a bit flat, so to give mine some permanent height I designed some triangular rope supports in L-shaped beds at the corners. They have proved very practical, with hairy, synthetic hemp-like rope giving good grip to beans and sweet peas, and they look good even when not being used. I chose this synthetic rope because it not only looks natural but also provides years of service in the garden.

1. Sturdy posts slot into the corners of the beds using a clever half joint cut by a carpenter.

2. To add stability, a couple of screws pass through the posts into the edge of the frame. Pre-drilling the holes makes this easier.

3. Holes are drilled at regular intervals on the edge
   of the frame and vertical posts, and ropes go from
   one side of the frame through the post to the other,
   keeping the rope taut.

# Filling the Beds

1. Fill the beds with a mixture of topsoil, well-rotted manure, and compost before the gravel paths are put down, as this is inevitably a messy job. If drainage is likely to be a problem, the area below the bed will need some work (see page 18).

2. As a rough guide, add one wheelbarrow of organic matter for every barrowful of topsoil used.

3. Add the soil and organic matter in thin layers. Spread them out and avoid compacting them too firmly.

4. Fill the beds to just below the top edge—the soil level will fall naturally as the soil settles. The beds are now ready for planting. I also spread a 2–3 in. (5–7.5 cm) layer of local gravel over the weed-suppressing landscape fabric and the paths.

# Adding to My Vegetable Patch

I built my original vegetable plot in early spring since I gardened in that season and decided I could cope with more. Initially, I thought I would neither want nor have the time to grow bulk crops such as potatoes, onions, and leeks, so I went for small, neat raised beds, but I found I could take on more space and the idea of some larger beds appealed to me. So the following spring I created large beds measuring 5 x 18 ft. (1.5 x 5.5 m) outside the protective fencing, in the shape of a capital E. I reasoned that if I chose what I grew here wisely the wildlife might not be an issue. So far this has worked well with onions, garlic, potatoes, and leeks. For other crops I give temporary protection (see pages 184–187).

The new beds gave me a burst of enthusiasm and the chance to grow a lot more produce, including cut flowers. This was more work and I tolerated a few more weeds, but the rewards were worth the effort. The following spring I added three more large beds the mirror image of the first, separated from them by a gravel area with herbs planted in pots and a large gazing ball. This gave me yet more space, more work, and a little more chaos but the garden still works well. Sometimes it is not that neat, things do occasionally get out of hand, and my raspberries may spend a few weeks sharing their bed with buttercups or the zucchinis (courgettes) with the occasional nettle, but they all get dealt with eventually and the harvests of truly succulent, nutritious fruits and vegetables are still excellent.

▶ My low-maintenance vegetable garden in early summer.

# Irrigation Systems

Although I advocate watering wisely for a whole range of reasons (see pages 180–181), there are times when watering is an unavoidable necessity and a time-consuming chore. Pottering around with a watering can on a summer's morning can be enjoyable, but if you are a time-poor gardener or someone who has to leave the garden to fend for itself for long periods then it's just not possible. A great many crops can be left without water, but recently planted transplants (plug plants) or young seedlings need to be pampered a little and given ample water to help them get established. A very simple automatic irrigation system is the solution. Components are available from DIY stores or online and simply push together to form a system tailor-made for your plot. It is important that the system is equipped with a basic timer so you can set it for as long as is necessary and that the delivery nozzles can be turned off, since you will not need to irrigate the whole garden all the time.

The timing device attaches to a series of black plastic hoses that run around the garden and through each bed, and T-pieces and L-shaped connectors mean that you can make the shapes you need and divide the hoses if necessary. Narrow feeder tubes can then be joined to the main hose and an appropriate dripper or nozzle. The main hoses can easily be hidden under the gravel or paths. A simpler option is a length of soaker hose that can be attached to a timer and moved around from bed to bed as needed. However you build your system, you must have the ability to turn areas off as you will rarely, if ever, want to water everything at the same time. Realistically, you will need to review what is getting watered at least every one or two weeks.

There are some more traditional and homespun methods of giving thirsty crops like the zucchinis (courgettes), cucumbers, and pumpkins a constant supply of water. One of these is based on ollas and is traditionally used in South America. These are large, bulb-shaped terracotta pots buried in the ground at the center of a bed with the mouth just showing. The pot is filled with water, and as the plants and evaporation remove water from the surrounding soil, the water seeps through the body of the porous pot to replace it. Very simple, yet very effective.

▲ The force of the water flowing through this nozzle causes it to spin, delivering water over a wide area. This is not a good choice if large leaves will stop the water from reaching the soil.

◄ A simple nozzle that can be turned on and off delivers water to a small area at soil level, so little is lost.

## Making a Simple Irrigation System

A simple olla system can be made using two large terracotta flowerpots as follows:

1. Close the drainage hole in one pot using a piece of tile and silicone sealant.
2. Place a generous amount of silicone sealant around the top of the rim of one pot and balance the second pot on the sealant so the rims match perfectly. Leave it to dry overnight.
3. Dig a hole in the center of the area to be irrigated large enough to accommodate both pots and set the pots in the hole so that the open drainage hole is uppermost. Backfill the hole so that the base of the pot is about 1 in. (2.5 cm) above the soil.
4. Water the bed well and fill the olla—a funnel may be helpful. Top up whenever the water level is low.

# THE BASICS

If you are short on time, can only visit your plot occasionally, or need to leave your plot unattended for long periods of time, then install a basic automatic irrigation system.

Everything you need is available from DIY stores or online.

Research the available components and draw up a basic plan before buying.

▼ Two terracotta pots joined by a generous layer of silicone sealant to form a single vessel.

▼ The joined pots are buried in the soil where needed with just the top showing an inch or so above the soil.

# Planning

Carefully planning what to grow and where to grow it is just as important for making your vegetable patch efficient as planning your garden. This kind of planning is invaluable for beginners and experienced vegetable growers alike.

## Planning What to Grow

The ideal time to plan what to grow is in late winter, before things in the garden are stirring. It is always exciting to leaf through seed catalogs and fire up your enthusiasm for another year in the garden. The detail of which crops are a good option for the low-maintenance vegetable garden is covered in What to Grow starting on page 42, but it is worth considering the principle and value of having a plan here.

Make a realistic list of what you would like to grow. Use a photocopy of your garden layout plan to mark what you plan to grow where—this will help to curb over-ordering and ensures you have space for everything. The listings on pages 48–161 give guidance on how much space you might want to allot to each crop and should be used as a very rough guide to help you out until you gain experience. Once you have made this list, stick to it. It is easy to be seduced by colorful seed packets, unusual varieties, or perky young plants at the garden center or nursery but try to resist. I have succumbed to such temptations and regretted it since I try to shoehorn in this unnecessary indulgence.

If it is your first year, leave space in your plan for the permanent plants that will produce year after year. Choose their location carefully and consider the shade that tall plants, such as raspberries, might cast over neighboring beds.

The most time-effective way to deal with obtaining plants and seeds is by mail order. Seed catalogs and the Internet have a wealth of varieties available and solid information. You can place your order early in the year and plants and seeds should arrive at your door in good time to get them in the ground. If you get it right this is a once-a-year task.

◀ If you plan and place a mail order early in the year, young plants, like these leeks, arrive at your door carefully packaged, ready to plant out at just the right time of year.

▶ A sturdy box with index cards and a lid is a practical way to keep seed packets tidy.

# Making Lists

A vegetable garden notebook is invaluable. Each year I begin with a list of the plants and seeds I have ordered, and a plan of where I aim to grow them is always tucked in the back, along with the plans from previous years. The other important list is an inventory of every variety of any crop I have ever grown with comments. It is a handy reminder of what has done well, what has tasted particularly good, and, most importantly, what has failed to thrive. When I plan my order at the beginning of the year, a glance at this list makes life easier. While it is always fun to try new varieties, it is good to have the guaranteed bumper harvest of proven favorites.

This notebook can also record a timetable for repeat sowing of crops to ensure an extended harvest and tasks to be done. Often when you have a short time in the garden, the valuable first ten minutes can be spent deciding what to do or a whole 30 minutes can pass by with a bit of general, pleasurable pottering and nothing worthwhile achieved, so my notebook holds a sort of rolling "things to do" list, which I update each time I garden, so, in theory at least, vital tasks get done. It sounds a bit rigid, but if I have 20 minutes and I know peas need sowing, strawberries need straw around them, and the onions need hoeing, it seems to get done. By midsummer the list gets very short and most of my time in the garden is spent picking vegetables, which is much nicer than time spent in the supermarket.

## THE BASICS

Keep a simple notebook with lists of plants ordered.

Use it to plan your time and keep track of repeat sowing.

▲ If you are a busy person, crops that need repeat sowing are easily forgotten, so a simple list of what to sow when is invaluable. This second batch of peas is being sown just a few weeks after the first; as the first batch finishes producing, the second should begin.

▶ A vegetable garden notebook and a basic plan of what is going to grow where help the vegetable plot to run efficiently.

# PART II

# What to Grow

Choosing what to grow is one of the key factors for a successful
and easily managed vegetable garden. Some crops are tolerant
and easygoing and will reward little care with a bumper harvest
of great-tasting vegetables. Others are prima donnas who have
particular demands that must be met, often at great effort, for them
to produce successfully, and there are plenty that fall in between.
Since we are looking for the maximum reward for the minimum
effort the prima donnas are out (unless, of course, they are your
favorite and worth the fuss, at the expense of growing other
things). One cultivar of a plant may be much easier to grow than
another, either in general or specifically because of the conditions
in your garden. It is far easier to choose plants that will thrive in
your particular circumstances than face the challenge of a relentless
battle to provide what a particular plant requires. For example,
peppers and eggplants (aubergines) will struggle in colder areas
without protection and perhaps artificial heat, so may not be an
option if your vegetable plot is cooler and exposed.

# Choosing What to Grow

Your vegetable garden is all about providing you with great things to eat, so start by listing all those fruits and vegetables that your family will enjoy feasting on, things that will make the project worthwhile. There is a common vision of vegetable plots with orderly ranks of parsnips, runner beans, rutabagas (swedes), and leeks and a tendency to think that your patch should include these. The reality is that if you are putting your precious time into growing something it should be a vegetable that's a staple in your kitchen and something you will eagerly anticipate harvesting.

Once you have made your list check the ease with which things are grown and the suitability for your plot. There are some crops that I don't recommend in a low-maintenance plot, unless you are fanatical about them and are willing to take on the challenge of growing them (see pages 46–47). The second consideration is how much space you need to dedicate to each crop to get a good harvest. Each entry in the listings on pages 48–161 gives a good idea of this. Ask yourself if there is space in your plot. If you only want to maintain a small space, then plants with a big space requirement, however easy to grow, may be unsuitable. Statuesque artichokes, for example, may deliver a gourmet crop, but each plant will probably deliver two or three suppers each year and occupy 11 square feet (1 square meter) of your plot, permanently. Third, look at when you can expect to harvest each crop; if you are away for long periods, it would be a shame to miss the best of anything.

Below are three lists detailing the "very easy to grow," the "easy to grow," and the "fairly easy to grow." Those in the first list are forgiving plants that will reward very little care and even neglect with basket-loads of flavorful produce. The second-list plants are just a little more demanding of your time or conditions, but certainly not a challenge—in most cases what makes them more difficult than those in the first list is the need to protect them from pests or their need for water. The third category need a bit more fuss. Much of the fruit falls into the second category purely because it requires pruning, although it has the advantage of being a permanent fixture.

Complete beginners and those really wanting very little to do would do well to grow plenty of things from the "very easy" list and have a really rewarding first season.

## How Easy Are They to Grow?

### Very Easy

- Potatoes
- Zucchinis (courgettes)
- Onions and shallots
- Rhubarb
- Runner beans
- Jerusalem artichokes
- Leeks
- Spring onions
- Perpetual spinach

### Easy

- Kale
- Pumpkins and squashes
- Salad leaves
- Radishes
- Garlic
- Artichokes
- Celeriac
- Peas and snow peas (mangetout)
- Strawberries
- Black currants
- Blackberries
- Gooseberries
- Raspberries
- Red currants
- Asparagus
- Beets (beetroot)

### Fairly Easy

- Carrots
- Broccoli and calabrese
- Green beans (French beans)
- Cabbage
- Fava beans (broad beans)
- Sweet corn
- Swiss chard
- Lettuce
- Tomatoes
- Peppers and chili peppers
- Cucumbers
- Eggplants (aubergines)

# Choosing Which Cultivar to Grow

Growing your own is all about great flavors, so always, always go for cultivars known for their great taste. Beyond this there are a number of characteristics to look for that will really cut down your workload and ensure bumper harvests. The listings on pages 48–161 suggest a few well-proven varieties to try, but there are new selections available every year. Seed catalogs and seed packets are marketing tools, but good ones are also crammed with information about how varieties are likely to perform.

## What to Look For

Look for prolific production over a long period of time. It is common sense that if one plant will give you 10 percent more vegetables than another or will deliver vegetables for several weeks longer, then you are getting better value for your time and money.

Resistance to pests and diseases is also an important factor to consider. Tending a crop for weeks, eagerly anticipating a fantastic harvest, only to find it ravaged by pests or ruined by disease is incredibly disappointing. So it is not surprising that a great deal of effort has gone into developing plants that will not suffer attacks from common pests and diseases. Protecting crops from things like carrot fly and cabbage root fly, for example, is time consuming and not always effective, so choosing cultivars with built-in resistance really makes sense, especially if you have experienced a problem before. Unfortunately, resistance does not mean complete and guaranteed immunity.

▲ One of the easiest crops to grow, onions require no care beyond weeding to give a great harvest.

◄ The zucchini (courgette) cultivar 'Orelia' gives a remarkably bountiful harvest of nutritious yellow fruits.

## Flavor

The exact taste of the produce you grow will be dependent on many things: the variety, of course, but soil, climate, and watering all have a part to play. Fruits grown in direct sunlight are likely to be sweeter and the more water some crops receive, the more diluted the flavor is. There can even be a variation between plants. I have two 'Oregon Thornless' blackberry plants that are only 10 ft. (3 m) apart, yet one produces the most fragrant, sweet berries, while the berries from the other, though they look the same, are only fit for cooking. So, although a variety is renowned for its superlative flavor, this might not be true in your garden; you may need to experiment with what works.

## Permanent Productive Planting

Probably the ultimate in achieving the best recompense for endeavor, the permanent plants in the vegetable garden are the ultimate low-maintenance, productive plants. The most time-economical plot would consist just of perennials and fruit. The range is obviously limited, but for the most part the plants will produce year after year with just a good layer of mulch in spring and perhaps a quick prune. The plants are more expensive at the outset, but the longevity negates this cost and the bit of extra effort that has to go into planting to give them a great start. An asparagus bed could last for ten years, so it is worth including at least some permanent occupants in the plan for your plot.

# What Not to Grow

Everyone has their own personal "what not to grow" list based on experience and dislikes. I once even read of someone who would not grow peas and another who found homegrown onions no better than those in stores. I couldn't disagree more. Succulent peas, fresh from the pod, are one of the most popular treats on my vegetable plot, grazed regularly by my children, so popular in fact few make it to the table. I find homegrown onions superior in flavor and sheer juiciness, and are such a staple in my kitchen I couldn't do without them. The climate and soil you have will also play a part in determining which plants will flourish and which will take extra work to coax them to produce a decent crop.

Here are the things I would suggest not growing unless they are a particular favorite.

## Rutabagas (Swedes)

There are several reasons not to grow rutabagas (swedes)—their growing season is long and they will occupy space from early spring right through to late

▲ Although they need 11 square feet (1 square meter) of garden space all year round and have a short season, artichokes are really easy to grow and a great treat for their fans.

▲ Planted as container-grown plants or bare-root after the first year, rhubarb will provide plenty of tasty stems for just a good layer of mulch once a year.

autumn and winter. It is true that they can be harvested at a lean time in the garden, but at that time they are inexpensive at the store and the flavors for me are just not that different.

## Cauliflower

There are some fantastically appealing cauliflower

cultivars, but to grow a good cauli you have to be pretty exact with feeding and watering if they aren't to bolt (send up flower spikes).

## Spinach

The problem with spinach is that it is so prone to bolting (sending up flower spikes) if conditions are not absolutely right. A much better option is to grow spinach beet, often known as perpetual spinach. The leaves can be cooked and the young leaves used in salads just like spinach. It will produce for at least a year and maybe more, even lightly through the winter in mild areas. It is a versatile food that really earns its keep. There are those who would point out its lack of spinach's delicacy, but for the most part this really doesn't matter!

## Celery

Growing good celery is very difficult. It requires a constant level of moisture in the soil—the slightest period of drying out and it won't perform. Celery also needs extremely good, fertile soil and regular feeding throughout the growing period. Most cultivars need each plant to be provided with a newspaper or cardboard collar secured with string around its stems and then the plants need "earthing up" three times to blanch the stems. On top of all this, slugs and snails love them. Celeriac offers a similar flavor for much, much less effort, and it can be grated in salads, roasted, or used in casseroles.

## Florence Fennel

The delicate flavor of fennel would earn it a place in the vegetable garden were it not for the exacting conditions it requires. It is not hard work to grow, but any challenging conditions and it will bolt and, once this has happened, it is inedible. Lack of water, root disturbance, poor soil conditions, changes in temperature, or cold nights could all cause it to bolt. To get tender stems the plants require "earthing up."

## Eggplants (Aubergines) and Peppers in Cold Areas

Both of these plants are reasonably straightforward to cultivate if you have the right climate or a greenhouse, as they need a fair amount of heat over a reasonably long summer to produce a worthwhile harvest. If you garden in a cold climate, you may be able to get a decent harvest by growing the plants in pots in a sunny spot sheltered by the house. Eggplants (aubergines) hail from tropical climes, so it is not surprising that they should struggle in a chilly, damp environment.

## Summer Squash (Marrows)

Growing a good summer squash (marrow) needs much the same conditions as growing good zucchinis (courgettes), and they are very straightforward. However, they take up quite a bit of space for the reward and unremarkable flavors. Each plant needs about 11 square feet (1 square meter) and will deliver only two or three summer squash (marrows) (any further flowers have to be removed to get fair-sized fruits). For me, they are not a great treat to eat and the flavors of homegrown and supermarket summer squash (marrows) are much the same.

## Vining (Cordon) Tomatoes

Rather than growing vining, or cordon, tomatoes (the upright plants that require support and regular tying-in, as well as their side shoots pinching out and trusses removing) it is far simpler to grow outdoor bush tomatoes that require none of the effort and give an excellent crop of magical, fragrant tomatoes.

# Dealing with Shade

Choosing what to grow wisely also requires assessing the limitations of your plot. Dealing with shade is one of the toughest problems to face, since most fruit and vegetables will do best in a sunny, sheltered spot. Deep shade is usually impossible to work with, but if your plot is partially shaded there are plants that will produce reasonably well. Trying to coax sun lovers to produce is probably a waste of resources. Fruiting plants generally need at least six hours of direct sunlight during the growing season. Root crops may tolerate less, but leafy vegetables are the best option for a partially shaded spot as scorching sun can actually damage delicate leaves.

**Plants That Will Tolerate Partial Shade**
- Perpetual spinach
- Summer cabbages
- Spring onions
- Radishes
- Salad greens
- Gooseberries
- Chard
- Jerusalem artichokes (will grow just about anywhere)
- Red and black currants
- Rhubarb
- Peas and beans (only very light shade)

# PART III

# Low-Maintenance Vegetables

✦ ✦ ✦ Very Easy   ✦ ✦ ✧ Easy

✦ ✧ ✧ Fairly Easy

# Salads and Greens

**Perpetual Spinach (Spinach Beet) • Swiss Chard • Lettuce • Salad Leaves**

# Perpetual Spinach (Spinach Beet) ✶ ✶ ✶

Delivering exceptional value for its space in the garden, spinach beet will provide a succulent crop of leaves for salads or cooking, from not long after planting through the following spring, with only the minimum of care. A whole year of productivity from one set of plants! It is an obliging plant used in place of spinach, a few leaves being harvested from several plants each time. In fact, it is one of those wonderful plants that reward regular harvesting with yet more tender leaves. Spinach beet is a tidy grower, especially when picked regularly, and can be used to edge beds. It has the reputation of being a poor man's spinach; maybe the leaves don't look as tempting as spinach, but they taste good, cook well, and just keep growing in more temperate areas even through winter when spinach won't grow, and will deliver a great crop on dry soils where spinach would run to seed! A perfect beginner's crop that will also grow well in a container.

▲ These young plants have already provided several harvests and will go on to produce tasty leaves for months to come.

### Varieties to Try
Named varieties are rarely available.

### Plant or Seed?
Plants.

### Spacing and Planting
6 in. (15 cm) between plants, 12 in. (30 cm) between rows. Stagger plants. Grows well in blocks.

### When to Plant
Mid-spring.

### When to Harvest
Early summer, just a few weeks after planting depending on weather conditions.

### How Many?
Twenty plants should give a good harvest.

### Repeat Sowing
No.

### Ideal Conditions
Very unfussy.

### Maintenance
Pick a few leaves from each plant regularly, but start by picking lightly so plants get well established. In temperate areas, they will grow through the winter without protection but in some areas the ferocity of the weather may damage the leaves, so to avoid this they can be protected by floating row covers (fleece).

### When to Water
Will withstand dry soil but rewards watering in very dry spells.

### Common Problems and Solutions
None of note.

# Swiss Chard ★ ✩ ✩

With large, crinkled leaves and thick, colorful stems, midribs, and veins, Swiss chard may be unfamiliar since it is one of those crops that can only really be enjoyed at its best if you grow your own. It soon wilts once harvested and isn't often available to buy. Picked young, the leaves can be cooked whole, but larger leaves need the tough stems removed before cooking. These can either be composted or cooked separately. Young leaves with their bright stems liven up a green salad.

### Varieties to Try

**Swiss chard,** sometimes known as Silver chard, has deep green leaves and thick white stems. It reaches about 20 in. (50 cm) high and is the most productive and robust of the chards.

**'Northern Lights'** has a mixture of brightly colored, shining stems that always strike me as slightly artificial. This chard will certainly add a burst of color to the garden, though it is not such a strong grower as the less flashy Swiss chard.

**Ruby chard,** as its name suggests, has glowing, ruby-red stems and its leaf is a very dark green, making it a real eye-catcher. Like 'Northern Lights' it is easy to grow but won't deliver as much leafy greens as Swiss chard. Very ornamental and will grow well in containers.

### Plant or Seed?

Transplants or small plants.

### Spacing and Planting

8 in. (20 cm) between plants, 16 in. (40 cm) between rows. Stagger plants.

### When to Plant

Late spring.

### When to Harvest

Start cutting the leaves, a few from each plant, as soon as they are large enough to use. As the stems are quite thick, you will need to cut them with a knife rather than picking or pulling them. They can be harvested until cut down by the frost, but even then if left in the ground they may regrow a little in the spring. At any time they can be cut to the ground and will sprout a crop of succulent baby leaves.

### How Many?

Twenty plants.

### Repeat Sowing

No.

### Ideal Conditions

Very unfussy.

### Maintenance

Pick regularly to ensure plenty of new leaves. Large, coarse, or battered leaves aren't worth eating—instead, put them on the compost pile.

### When to Water

In dry spells.

### Common Problems and Solutions

Protect small plants from slugs and snails if they are a problem in your garden (see page 185).

▶ A few of these succulent young leaves can be taken from each plant and used in salads.

# Lettuce ★ ✩ ✩

There is an astounding range of lettuces available to grow in your vegetable garden with an amazing range of leaf shapes and colors, from frilly red to crisp green and undulating bronze. They are the backbone of summer salads, looking equally attractive in the garden as on the plate. I like to have some fun with the planting of lettuces, alternating contrasting leaf shapes, forms, and colors, and adding in a few marigolds to make a very pretty bed. There are cultivars recommended for growing over the winter months, although since these aren't easy to manage, it is better to choose one of the host of other salad greens that are more reliable. I have planted beds of overwintering varieties, given them all the protection I could muster, and still the plants have been lost. Summer lettuces take up little time and thrive if the soil and watering are right. Choosing varieties that work well as a cut-and-come-again crop suits the low-maintenance gardener because it means you can have a constant supply of sensational small leaves for salads and sandwiches from just one planting, which is perfect when you are trying to save time.

## Varieties to Try •

'**Can Can**' is a green non-hearting lettuce with sweet, crisp, frilly leaves suitable as a cut-and-come-again crop. It also has good disease resistance.

'**Salad Bowl**' is a large, fast-growing cut-and-come-again lettuce that should produce leaves for a whole season. Slow to bolt.

'**Pinokkio**' is a short romaine-type lettuce that produces a good heart and is resistant to downy mildew.

'**Sentry**' has very decorative, wavy-edged, reddish leaves and can be used as a single head or as cut-and-come-again. It has a good resistance to mildew.

'**Fristina**' is a reliable oak-leaved variety with a good flavor.

'**Little Gem**' is a small hearting lettuce that produces crisp, pale hearts. It is fast-growing and compact, so though you do have to wait for the heart to form, you don't have to wait long! Don't be tempted to grow too many hearting lettuces because they will all be ready at about the same time.

'**Lollo Rossa**' is a lavishly frilly, Italian non-hearting lettuce that can be harvested as a cut-and-come-again crop. It is a wonderfully attractive plant with a great taste.

## Plant or Seed?
Plants and later sowing of seed.

## Spacing and Planting
Plants can be set as close as 4 in. (10 cm) for small varieties or 10 in. (25 cm) for larger.

## When to Plant
Late spring.

## When to Harvest
Start picking a few leaves as soon as the plants are large enough. Always pick just one or two leaves from each plant, leaving at least four or five at the center. In the summer each plant will rapidly regenerate, slightly more slowly in the spring and autumn. Eventually the lettuce will bolt and the plant can be removed.

◀ Eaten just moments after it is picked, homegrown lettuce retains all of its crisp juiciness and bite.

## How Many?

Twenty plants.

## Repeat Sowing

I start the season with a selection of cut-and-come-again plants, and once these have been producing for a while, I try to direct sow a selection of lettuces to take their place. This way the whole season is covered.

## Ideal Conditions

Lettuces enjoy a rich soil that is not compacted.

## Maintenance

Young plants can be affected by competition from weeds, but if they are planted close together they will soon cover the ground.

## When to Water

Lettuces need regular watering to thrive, but it is important to water the soil and not the leaves as they can be damaged and rot.

## Common Problems and Solutions

**Slugs and snails** love tender lettuce leaves and are a particular threat to seedlings and young plants. Larger plants are able to withstand a little damage. Use the methods outlined on page 185 to protect your crop. **Aphids** (greenfly) are particularly unpleasant if they are plentiful. It takes real dedication to wash them out of deeply frilly leaves and, to be honest, as my mother says, who wants their food secondhand? This problem can be avoided by growing lettuces under a floating row cover (fleece) or fine insect-proof mesh from the outset. **Bolting** can be a problem in hot weather or if watering is inconsistent. Generally the leaves of plants that bolt are bitter and inedible, and should be composted.

▶ Picking a few leaves from a number of plants makes for an interesting salad and means that one plant will produce for weeks.

# Salad Leaves ✦ ✦ ✧

Salad leaves are close to effortless to grow; just sprinkle the seed, water, and wait. Sometimes they can be picked after only three or four weeks, because the plants start producing long before they are mature. There is a plethora of plants that can be grown and you can very easily produce an enormous variety of salad leaves with a whole range of exciting tastes, colors, and textures—there is no excuse for a boring salad. Many of the leaves are from immature plants such as kale or beets (beetroot), or a mix of oriental greens such as komatsuna, mizuna, Chinese cabbage, and mustard greens. The simplest way to go about growing an interesting mix of salad leaves, especially for the beginner, is to try some of the mixed packets of seed on the market. Many are ready for eating in just a few weeks and will contain a vast array of different and interesting plants. Some are themed, promising spicy leaves, fast growing varieties, or a winter mix, and most can be treated as a cut-and-come-again crop, so you can pick from each plant a number of times. Add a few snippets of fresh herbs and some colorful edible flowers and you have something infinitely superior to those sold in sealed bags. They grow well in containers, and I have even grown them in a vast bowl in the center of the kitchen table.

## Varieties to Try

Any salad leaf mix. Or create your own by mixing packets of seeds of your favorite leaf lettuces.

## Plant or Seed?

Seed.

## Spacing and Planting

Sow thinly in shallow, wide furrows about ⅜ in. (1 cm) deep. Thinning out is not necessary. Mixed salad leaves can be broadcast (sprinkled over the soil in a wide area rather than in straight rows). This is an efficient use of space, and pretty, too. In reality, when the plants initially come up they are indistinguishable from weeds, especially if they are new to you, so neat lines make it easier to see what needs to be weeded out. I always sow into a layer of seed starting mix.

## When to Sow

Depending on the varieties chosen, from early spring through to early autumn.

## When to Harvest

As soon as the leaves look large enough to enjoy you can start harvesting, probably when they are about 4 in. (10 cm) high. Use scissors to snip the leaves or pinch them from the plants. Alternatively, when the plants are about 4–6 in. (10–15 cm) tall the whole plant can be cut to about 2 in. (5 cm) above ground level as needed. Within three to four weeks there should be another harvest ready and another about four weeks after that.

## How Many?

Probably a quarter to half a packet of seed at one time.

## Repeat Sowing

Yes, plant a new batch of seeds just before you start harvesting the first and so on.

## Ideal Conditions

Moist, rich soil.

## Maintenance

Keep weeds down, especially when plants are young.

## When to Water

Salad leaves are one crop where you really cannot hold back on the watering as they need a constantly moist soil to grow well. Water the soil, not the plants—a soaker hose works well.

## Common Problems and Solutions

**Insect pests** including aphids (greenfly) and flea beetle are likely to be the most significant problems depending on the mix of leaves you are growing. Both can be kept from the plants by growing them under a floating row cover (fleece) or the finest insect-proof mesh in the summer months.

**Slugs and snails** will also enjoy the lush leaves. Use the methods outlined on page 185 to protect your crop.

◀ This mix of leaves, including mizuna, mustard leaves, and arugula (rocket), will deliver a good mix of tastes, textures, and colors.

▶ It is tough to distinguish weed from plant at this stage, so it pays to sow seeds in neat bands or rows.

# Podded Vegetables

**Peas and Snow Peas (Mangetout) • Green Beans (French Beans)**
**Borlotti Beans • Runner Beans • Fava Beans (Broad Beans)**

# Peas and Snow Peas (Mangetout) ★ ★ ✗

Eating juicy peas straight from the pod is one of the great treats in the vegetable garden and those that make it to the table are no less succulent. Peas fresh from the garden are nothing like those in the stores—as soon as peas are picked the sugars that make them so delicious start becoming starches, and while frozen peas may be OK, they are nowhere near as good. Peas grow well, but keeping up a constant supply needs planning and space—perhaps better to make two or three sowings and have the harvest in bursts of a few weeks at a time. The most labor intensive part of growing peas is the shelling, and although I often find that I have plenty of volunteers for this, not as many peas as anticipated make it to the saucepan. Growing snow peas (mangetout) cuts out the work of shelling as the pods are tender and eaten in their entirety, although they can get stringy if left on the plant too long. Shelling peas are either wrinkle- or round-seeded—the round varieties are generally hardier and the wrinkled varieties are generally thought to be sweeter.

▲ The young tips of the pea plant can be added to salads. Harvest just a few at a time so as not to ruin your crop of peas.

## Varieties to Try

'Kelvedon Wonder' is one of my favorites. It can be planted from early spring through early summer, so there is no need to buy more than one variety of pea. It is a shelling variety that produces a bumper crop of pods crammed with good-sized and sweet-tasting peas that are quick to mature. It also has the advantage of being mildew resistant, growing to about 20 in. (50 cm) tall.

'Hurst Green Shaft' is worth trying; it also produces a heavy crop of sweetly flavored peas and promises good disease resistance. This is a taller variety, growing to about 30 in. (75 cm) and is a main crop cultivar.

'Onward' is another main crop variety, and also offers some disease resistance and a good flavor. Grows to about 1 yd. (1 m) in height.

'Little Marvel' is a very sweet dwarf pea, only reaching about 17 ¾ in. (45 cm) tall, but it produces a wonderful harvest very early in the year.

'Oregon Sugar Pod' is a great, fast-maturing variety of snow peas (mangetout). When gathered young, the pods are crisp and fleshy and great in salads, stir-fries, or steamed.

## Plant or Seed?
Seed.

## Spacing and Planting

Direct sow early varieties from mid-spring in wide furrows about 8 in. (20 cm) wide with two or three rows of peas so that the peas are about 2 in. (5 cm) away from each other. Leave about 18–24 in. (45–60 cm) between rows for the shorter varieties. Alternatively, if you are working in small beds, sow a block of peas aiming at about 8–10 seeds per square foot (30 square centimeters), although remember you will need to be able to reach into the center of the block to harvest the peas.

## When to Sow

Early varieties can be sown from early spring, while main crops can be sown from mid- to late spring. Some varieties are very hardy and can be sown in the autumn to produce a crop very early the following year, although I have never found this to be worthwhile because the ground is cold and damp and the seed is liable to rot. Mice and birds are hungry, so are likely to eat the seed, and some protection may well be needed. Better to wait a little longer and not waste time or seed.

## When to Harvest

The first peas of cultivars sown in the early spring should be ready in early summer, about 10–12 weeks after sowing. Pick snow peas (mangetout) as soon as pods are about 1 ½ in. (4 cm) long, because old snow peas (mangetout) are tough and stringy.

## How Many?

One 6 ½–10 ft. (2–3 m) row each at sowing.

## Repeat Sowing

Sow two or three batches about three weeks apart, or when your previous sowing reaches 3–4 in. (7.5–10 cm) tall. Sow one batch of an early variety and one or two of a main crop, or make more sowings of 'Kelvedon Wonder.'

## Ideal Conditions

Peas appreciate a soil with plenty of organic matter. In cold, wet soil pea seeds tend to rot, so well-drained soil is necessary, especially for early sowings. Other than that peas are very unfussy and will even survive a little shade.

## Maintenance

All peas benefit from some support framework to grow through, even extremely short varieties. The easiest and nicest-looking are ranks of twiggy hazel or birch sticks pushed in along the rows of peas. These can be cut from woodlots or garden hedgerows or should be available from good garden centers. Plastic pea netting can also be bought at garden centers. This can be strung along the rows, but requires stout supports to keep it from drooping under the weight of the peas. Twigs are much easier and probably free. Once the plants are growing strongly they will tolerate a few weeds.

## Growing Peas and Snow Peas (Mangetout)

1. Pea seeds are a tasty treat for rodents. Dipping them in seaweed fertilizer before planting should help to protect the seeds from attack.

2. Sow peas in a flat-bottomed furrow about 8 in. (20 cm) wide in staggered rows so that the peas are about 2 in. (5 cm) apart, or grow them in a block with 8–10 seeds per 12 square in. (30 square cm).

## When to Water

When in flower and when pods are forming. Peas are one of the crops where knowing just when to water can save you time and water while maximizing your crop. Watering during flowering and while the pods are forming really boosts yields, but you can happily not water once the seedlings have emerged until flowering begins unless they wilt. Too much water before flowering encourages too much leafy growth.

## Common Problems and Solutions

Generally peas are trouble-free but there are just a couple of problems that can easily be avoided.

**Birds and mice** like to feast on pea seeds, although I have found they only bother unearthing the earliest sowings. After sowing, lay a piece of chicken wire over the soil to deter birds and rodents, or dip the seeds in seaweed fertilizer before planting to make them unpalatable to rodents.

**Mildew** is another common problem, especially in the autumn or dry periods, best avoided by sowing resistant varieties. It looks like a fine white powder or dust that starts at the tips of the leaves and will eventually cover the whole plant.

**Pea moth** can be a problem, and the most unpleasant thing that can happen to your long-awaited crop is to open the plump pods and find tiny maggots have gotten to them first! To avoid the problem sow only early and late as the pea moth lays its eggs on the flowers of plants that will produce midsummer, and the maggots then hatch and burrow their way into the pods. Alternatively, drape an insect barrier mesh over your crop once it comes into flower. If you find you are badly affected by pea moth, move your peas as far away as you can the following year, as the moth pupates in the soil.

3. When the pea plants begin to show, add hazel or birch twigs to provide support—this is much easier than constructing frames with netting.

4. Harvest peas when the pods fill out. Peas picked younger are much sweeter and completely delicious, although you get a much smaller harvest.

# Green Beans (French Beans) ✦ ✧ ✧

I always think of green beans (French beans) as the gourmet's alternative to the runner bean. They are inclined to be more tender, more flavorsome, and have the enormous benefit of being much easier to prepare. If I only had space to grow one type of bean I would choose to grow green beans (French beans). No stringing and slicing and plenty of taste. They are a little fussier than runner beans to grow, but not much. Climbing varieties are best as they give a bigger harvest for the space they occupy and produce for longer than the dwarf varieties, which can be useful in pots or on windy sites. Green bean (French bean) cultivars are available with purple and yellow pods, too.

▲ At this stage young bean plants can be killed overnight by slugs so a plastic bottle cloche is a good idea. Once they get a little bigger the odd nibble won't matter so much.

## Varieties to Try
**'Cobra'** is my favorite climbing green bean (French bean) cultivar. It produces a profusion of long, tender, stringless, pale pods with a good flavor right through to the autumn, as long as I keep picking them! It has a pretty purple flower, too.
**'Blue Lake'** is an older, reliable climbing variety that can be eaten whole or left on the plant so the seeds ripen to be used as haricots.
**'Purple King'** beans are a rich purple color while growing but, perhaps disappointingly, the color fades on cooking. Great flavor.

## Plant or Seed
Seed.

## Spacing and Planting
Plant seeds 2–4 in. (5–10 cm) apart and 2 in. (5 cm) deep, two at each station. Remove the weaker seedling if both germinate. If you are growing them up a cane tunnel, leave 24 in. (60 cm) between rows.

## When to Sow
Very late spring to early summer; the plants are not frost hardy and the seeds need a temperature of 54ºF (12ºC) to germinate.

## When to Harvest
You should start picking beans about 10–12 weeks from planting. Even if there are only a few ready, pick them to encourage the plants to produce more. If you want to use some beans as haricots, leave the pods on the plants for the beans to swell until the pods become brown and dry. This will halt the production of new pods, so use particular plants or wait until late in the season. It is easier to let this process take place on the plant naturally, but if the ripe pods are likely to suffer in very wet or frosty weather the pods can be dried inside.

▲ These 'Purple King' beans have a stunningly rich color that sadly fades when cooked.

## How Many?
Plant in 6 ½–10 ft. (2–3 m) rows.

## Repeat Sowing
Sow another batch about six to eight weeks after the first. To make life simpler, if the first planting is spaced a little more widely, the second batch can be planted among the first using the same support.

## Ideal Conditions
Good, rich soil with plenty of organic matter.

## Maintenance
Climbing beans need a framework or support to climb—canes, obelisks, or netting are fine. They will spiral around anything as they head skyward. Mulch around the plants once they are up to keep weeds down and preserve moisture—grass cuttings or newspaper will do.

## When to Water
Water when flowering starts if the weather is very dry to increase yields.

## Common Problems and Solutions
**Slugs** are the biggest and, in fact, the only problem I have had with green beans (French beans). To prevent the seedlings being completely eaten, I now plant each pair of seeds and immediately put a plastic bottle cloche over them, pushed well into the soil, to protect them.

The other likely hazard is being in too much of a hurry to get the seeds into the ground—they really don't like cold, damp conditions, and even if they come up the plants can rot.

# Borlotti Beans ★ ✧ ✧

If I were being rigorous in applying my principles about plants really earning their place in the vegetable plot, then I probably wouldn't be mentioning borlotti beans because the yield is comparatively small, but I mention them because they have the most startlingly gorgeous pods splashed with crimson and superb-tasting beans that make it worth growing just a few if you have the space. The growing requirements for borlotti beans are much like those for green beans (French beans) (see pages 65–66). 'Borlotto Lingua di Fuoco,' or 'Fire Tongue,' is the most common variety.

▶ The bright red flowers and dappled red pods of the borlotti bean make a colorful splash in the vegetable plot.

# Runner Beans ✶ ✶ ✶

One of the easiest veg to grow and one of the most likely crops to over-plant, the runner bean is one of those wonderful crops that will reliably produce abundantly and, if you plant too many, bring you to the point where you and everyone you know probably will be tired of eating them. They are a pleasure to have in the garden for their reliable profusion and colorful flowers, but beware of wasting precious time and space on sowing and tending too many, not to mention the time spent picking them! But don't let this put you off, just sow wisely, and a glut can of course be frozen. A very rewarding plant for the novice.

▲ Tendrils of 'Celebration' growing up a rope and the fully formed pods.

## Varieties to Try

**'Celebration'** is an early-maturing cultivar that produces a heavy crop of smooth tasty beans and has the added appeal of pretty salmon pink flowers. It is also resistant to rust.

**'Red Rum'** also matures early and promises a high yield of particularly fine-flavored beans. If you have trouble getting your bean flowers to set, this variety is worth trying as its flowers set extremely well, even in poor conditions. It is also resistant to Halo blight.

## Plant or Seed?
Seed.

## Spacing and Planting
Direct sow 2 in. (5 cm) deep and about 6–9 in. (15–23 cm) apart. Use two seeds at each station in case one fails to germinate and pull out one seedling if two grow. If growing beans up the traditional tunnel of sloping canes, allow at least 12 in. (30 cm) between rows.

## When to Sow
Runner beans need fairly warm soil to germinate, so wait until all risk of frosts have passed, probably in late spring.

## When to Harvest
You will probably harvest your first beans about 10–12 weeks from sowing. Regular picking encourages more pods to form.

## How Many?
I have already given dire warnings about over-planting so if you want beans to look forward to rather than dread, plant an 8 ft. (2.5 m) double row and see how it goes.

## Repeat Sowing
Possible but beware of over-planting.

## Ideal Conditions
Beans are a hungry crop; they need very rich soil with plenty of organic matter. Some gardeners labor all through the winter at filling a trench with waste in the spot they plan to grow their beans. This is not necessary if your soil is in good condition, just add plenty of organic material on planting. They will thrive on new beds created by deep-layer mulching (see pages 25–27).

## Maintenance
Runners need a framework to grow up. Traditionally, this is provided by two rows of 6 ½ ft. (2 m) canes or hazel rods about 12–24 in. (30–60 cm) apart sloping toward each other and tied at the top to a horizontal cane. I grow mine up a permanent framework of taut, hairy rope, although this means I need several to allow for crop rotation. Any type of obelisk will suffice. Pinch out the tips of the plants when they reach the top of the supports and mulch around the plants with compost or grass clippings to suppress weeds and keep in moisture. The most important thing is to keep picking. If you only visit your plot once a week, pick some beans slightly early to avoid them becoming old and unpalatable and ensure the production of new pods is not suppressed.

## When to Water
Runner beans are thirsty so water well throughout the season.

## Common Problems and Solutions
Runners are a robust crop and there is little to worry about.

**Failure to set**, where the flowers fail to develop into pods, is one of the commonest problems. If this seems to be an issue, step up the watering and mulch the bed to keep in moisture. This should help the pods form. It may be caused by a lack of pollinating insects, so in subsequent years add more companion planting to your plot or sow a few sweet peas among the beans (if you try this, take care not to harvest and eat the sweet pea pods).

**Halo blight** is something to look out for; this causes a pale ring on the leaves with a darker spot at its center. If you catch it early you can pinch off the affected leaves and destroy them, otherwise it can spread to the whole plant, eventually killing it. The alternative is to grow a resistant cultivar like 'Red Rum.'

# Fava Beans (Broad Beans) ✶ ✧ ✧

The humble fava bean (broad bean) is one of the earliest known cultivated crops; it earns its place in the veg patch today as it is the earliest of the beans to be ready for picking. Pick them while they are small and tender and they will be very different from the starchy, pithy beans found in the shops with pods that always look so old and battered. The older the beans the more starchy they become, but greedily enjoying lots of tiny beans makes for a smaller harvest. Being one of the earliest crops of the season it is well worth making space for a row, even if you just make the one sowing. There are plenty of other beans that will produce later in the season.

▲ A fine wire mesh pinned over newly planted bean seeds should prevent rodents getting to the seed before it germinates.

◀ Almost ready for harvest, these perfect pods of 'Aquadulce Claudia' will each contain about six or seven perfect beans.

## Varieties to Try

**'Aquadulce Claudia'** produces reliable, fantastic harvests of long pods. Reputed to be the best for autumn planting for early harvests.

**'The Sutton'** is a more compact, dwarf variety that can be planted with less space between rows. It can be sown in autumn or spring. Good for windy sites.

## Plant or Seed?
Seed.

## Spacing and Planting
Sow in double rows with 4 in. (10 cm) between seeds, 12 in. (30 cm) between rows, and 24 in. (60 cm) between double rows, 2 in. (5 cm) deep or in staggered rows with 6 in. (15 cm) between each seed.

## When to Sow
There are two planting periods for fava beans (broad beans): one in autumn to early winter, the other in early spring through to the beginning of summer. Planting in the autumn makes for sturdy plants that are less attractive to blackfly. The young plants are pretty tough, surviving down to 14°F (-10°C) if the seed doesn't rot in the ground or get devoured by hungry rodents before it germinates. Plant in early spring and the plants get going faster. I have found that the autumn- and winter-sown beans have never proved worthwhile and so now stick to planting from very early spring. Later summer sowings are more prone to aphid attack and yields can be affected, so perhaps attempt just one or two sowings in spring when aphids are less troublesome.

## When to Harvest
The beans are ready when you can just see them through the pod, about 16 weeks from a spring planting.

## How Many?
In very good conditions a row of beans will produce 2 lb. (1 kg) per meter, so a couple of 6 ½ ft. (2 m) rows should be enough.

## Repeat Sowing
Possible, but after many attempts I have found sowing fava beans (broad beans) in the late autumn or winter for the following spring is not worthwhile, so I plant in very early spring and make perhaps a further sowing depending on how much space I have. Beyond this time, blackfly and chocolate spot just become too much of a problem and there are plenty of other things ready to harvest.

## Ideal Conditions
Fava beans (broad beans) give their best in deep, rich soils, but they will grow in poorer soils.

## Maintenance
There is really little to do with these rugged beans other than provide support for tall varieties in an exposed spot by creating a cage around them with posts and string or canes. Once the harvest is finished chop the tops off and leave the roots with the nitrogen-fixing nodules in the soil to benefit the plant that follows—the timing and nitrogen should suit brassicas.

## When to Water
Water in prolonged dry periods.

## Common Problems and Solutions
**Blackfly** is the biggest problem afflicting fava beans (broad beans)—they suck sap from the plant and cause it to weaken. The blackfly are drawn to the young sappy growth at the growing tips, so once the plant is in flower these tips can be pinched out to discourage the blackfly and serendipitously encourage pods to form.

**Chocolate spot** is a fungal disease that causes brown patches on the leaves of the plants. It can be prevented by improving drainage and ensuring plants are not too close together so air can circulate. Plants will continue to produce beans through a mild attack.

# Roots and Tubers

**Potatoes • Carrots • Radishes • Beets (Beetroot)
Jerusalem Artichokes**

# Potatoes ✶ ✶ ✶

Homegrown potatoes are simply delicious. There is nothing quite as satisfying as unearthing the multitude of tubers that form underground with so very little effort. Arguably, potatoes provide the tastiest reward to be had for the least work in the kitchen garden. The potato may seem like a humble basic, but the homegrown spud is so very good that its harvest is probably the most eagerly awaited by my whole family. There are many cultivars to choose from with something to suit all tastes, with different textures and skin colors to try—firm, waxy salad potatoes, fluffy ones that are great for mashing, and potatoes that will grow enormous for baking.

Potatoes fall into three categories depending on when they are ready to harvest: "first early" ready in June and July, "second early" ready for the table in July and August, and main crop potatoes, which follow on and can be stored through to the next spring. If you are short on time and space, it really isn't worth growing main crop potatoes—an early crop is a real treat and the flavors are exceptional, but main crop potatoes will occupy a lot of space when you could be growing other things, the homegrown taste is not so pronounced, and potatoes later in the season are inexpensive in the stores. Try to make space for at least a first early and, if you can, a second early variety and you won't regret it.

▲ There is nothing quite as satisfying as unearthing the multitude of tubers that form underground.

## Varieties to Try
### FIRST EARLY

'**Swift**' is the earliest potato of all, sometimes ready just seven weeks from planting! I have found the yield to be a little low, but the treat of digging potatoes so early is worth it, so I just plant a few. Its other great virtue is disease resistance.

'**Winston**' is a reliable producer with a great flavor every time I have grown it. I also like its versatility—it is a tasty new potato when dug early, but any left in the ground for a while bulk up into great baking potatoes.

'**Accent**' is slug resistant and provides a very good yield. Great both boiled and roasted.

### SECOND EARLY

'**Kestrel**' looks great with smooth tubers and patches of pinky purple. It has a good flavor and, perhaps best of all, it is resistant to slug damage. I have grown this cultivar when most everything else has been sampled by slugs and the 'Kestrel' spuds came through completely unscathed. This makes them an excellent choice where slugs ravage the garden.

'**Charlotte**' is a lovely, large salad potato with a waxy texture and an excellent flavor that is well worth growing. Unfortunately, the yields are not as good as 'Kestrel.'

'**Edzell Blue**' sports a puple or navy blue skin, making it fun to grow.

## Plant or Seed?

Potatoes are grown from seed potatoes, which ideally should be at least the size of a hen's egg and come from a reputable supplier to ensure they are disease free.

## Chitting

Before the seed potatoes are planted they should be encouraged to produce shoots—this is known as chitting. Simply lay the tubers out with the rose end (the end with lots of eyes) up in a cool, light, frost-free place so they can develop shoots. Once the shoots are about ⅝–1 in. (1.5–2.5 cm) long they can be planted. In my relentless quest to cut corners I have tried skipping this process, but the plants were much slower to get going, although the final harvest was fine.

## Spacing and Planting

Plant first early potatoes about 4 in. (10 cm) deep and 12 in. (30 cm) apart with 18 in. (45 cm) between rows. Second earlies and maincrop potatoes need a bit more space at 16 in. (40 cm) apart. The easiest way to plant is to scoop out a hole with a trowel (rather than dig a trench), drop in the seed potato with the shoots pointing upward, and cover with soil, being careful not to damage the brittle shoots as you cover them. Rub off any downward-facing shoots before planting. To get the spacing right, I generally lay all the seed potatoes out on the bed and then work my way along the row when planting. Cutting all the holes in the black plastic has the same effect (see page 77).

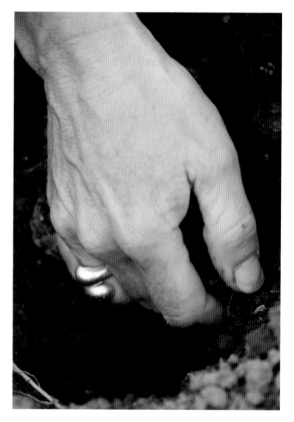

## Growing Potatoes

1. Lay out the chitted seed potatoes on the soil to ensure they are well spaced, preventing the last few from having to be squeezed in.

2. Some people like to dig a trench to plant potatoes in, but I find it easier to scoop out a small hole for each about 4 in. (10 cm) deep.

## When to Plant

Early to mid-spring, as early as possible. A good empirical indication of when to plant potatoes is when the grass and weeds start showing signs of growth. If a late frost is forecast, earth up the shoots or drape a piece of horticultural fleece over the bed to protect the young shoots. However, planting too early can mean tubers rot in the ground before they can grow.

## When to Harvest

Early cultivars can be ready as little as 60 to 70 days from planting, but as a general rule they are harvested when they finish flowering before the haulms (the stems and leaves) have died back. Dig them as you need them, but go carefully—it's always the choicest spuds that seem to end up impaled on my fork, and take care to dig out all the spuds. This is not just to avoid waste, but any tubers left in the ground will sprout the following year, annoyingly sticking their heads up among other crops.

## Repeat Sowing

A continuous supply is ensured by growing first and second early varieties and a main crop if required.

## Ideal Conditions

Potatoes are fairly easy-going and are often used as a crop on newly cleared ground because the process of earthing up and the bushy plants keep weeds down while the tubers open up the soil. A good soil rich with organic matter will yield the best crops, as potatoes are a very hungry crop. They do well in new deep-layer mulch beds (see pages 26–27).

3. Place the seed potato in the hole with the chits upward and carefully cover with soil.

4. Once the young plants are established they should be "earthed up," whereby the soil is dragged over the plant leaving just a little growth showing.

## Maintenance

Potatoes grown in the traditional way need earthing up—this simply means drawing the soil up around the plant to bury the shoots a few times as it grows. This prevents the potatoes coming to the surface and going green. Earthing up can also protect young shoots from late frosts. Earth up when the plants are about 6 in. (15 cm) high, or sooner if frosts are predicted, and again when there is another good 6 in. (15 cm) of growth showing.

## Shortcuts

A handy time-saving trick is to grow potatoes through black plastic sheeting. This serves many purposes; if it is put down a few weeks before planting, it will warm the soil and encourage early production, and it will suppress the weeds and avoid the need to earth up the potatoes. The down side is that it looks unattractive. The plastic is staked out over the soil and held down by burying the edges, or with planks or stones, and the potatoes are then planted through holes in the plastic.

An alternative is to grow potatoes under a mulch of straw and grass cuttings. This has the same advantages, perhaps looks a little more attractive, and can be used to clear new ground. A generous layer of compost is spread over the bed and the potatoes are set out on top. The potatoes are then covered with a thick duvet of straw. This can be topped up with grass cuttings as the potatoes grow. This method of growing potatoes can even be employed on a previously uncultivated area by cutting back any grass or weeds before the manure is spread and proceeding as above. To harvest the potatoes, just peel back the mulch of straw.

## When to Water

Earlies only need thorough watering every two weeks, if rainfall is not sufficient, to get the best yield possible. To make them produce earlier only water when the tubers are formed, around about when they flower—the crop will be early but small.

## Common Problems and Solutions

There are a several things that might threaten your potato crop, but many viruses can be avoided by buying in good-quality certified seed potatoes. Saving your own spuds to plant the following year may be thrifty, but it can lead to lower productivity and an increase in disease. If you want to try it, save seed from one year to the next, then buy seed potatoes in the third year.

**Blight** is a fungal disease that breaks out in cool, damp summers. The first signs are brown patches on the leaves and fungal rings on the underside of these patches; eventually the plants die back and can smell putrid. The best solution is to remove and destroy the tops, dig up the potatoes, and use them only if they are unaffected. Don't be tempted to put any of the foliage or potatoes on the compost heap, as you will just be storing up the problem to release it into the garden when you spread the compost. If blight is common in your area, grow blight-resistant varieties such as 'Milva,' 'Orla,' 'Karlena,' 'Spunta,' and the main crop 'Sarpo Mira.'

**Scab** causes small corky patches to appear on the skin of the potatoes. This is not a real problem as once peeled the potatoes are perfectly edible, but it can be a sign that your soil is drying out and could do with more organic matter.

**Keeled slugs** that live below the soil surface will eat into potatoes, causing rot to set in. If you have a problem with slugs, sow the marvelous slug-resistant variety "Kestrel."

It is worth mentioning that potatoes are one of the crops I have found to be untouched by deer, rabbits, and badgers when grown outside my protected area, presumably because of the toxicity of the foliage.

◀ The 'Kestrel' variety is resistant to slug damage and provides good-looking potatoes with plenty of tubers on each root.

# Carrots ★ ⚹ ⚹

Freshly dug, young, gloriously crisp, juicy carrots surpass any you will find in the shops—they just taste more like carrots. They give crunch and color to salads, are delicious steamed and even carefully roasted, but frankly they are so much better raw than cooked. They are a little more exacting than the potatoes and runner beans of the vegetable world, but by no means challenging.

◀ Globe carrots are a good solution in shallow or stony soils. They are popular with children, too.

## Varieties to Try

**'Purple Haze'** produces shockingly purple, good-sized carrots that keep their color even when cooked. Cut in rings, they have a purple band with an orange core. The color really appeals to children, and it's a little known fact that at one time all carrots were purple.

**'Paris Market'** is a globe-type carrot; it produces roundish roots that are excellent for snacking on once they reach the size of large marbles. This is another favorite among children because of its unusual shape. Its short root is an advantage in stony or heavy soils.

**'Autumn King 2'** is a solid, reliable cultivar with a rounded end. It is not as sweet and tender as some but stores well.

**'Maestro'** is resistant to carrot fly and has good-quality roots.

## Plant or Seed?
Seed.

## Spacing and Planting

Direct sow seed in furrows in soil worked to a fine tilth or a seed compost furrow (see page 172). Sow seeds in furrows ⅜ in. (1 cm) deep and about 8–10 in. (20–25 cm) apart, less for globe cultivars, and in the center of that gap I always plant a row of spring onions (if I am not planting in the onion bed—see page 81). Sow as thinly as possible in straight lines—this is tough because the seeds are tiny, but care here means no need to thin out seedlings later. The carrots inevitably come up in irregular knots and clusters but they push each other out of the way, and as soon as they are large enough to be eaten, some can be carefully taken from each group and the rest left to grow on. Not thinning out saves time and seeds but it also gives the carrot fly one less chance to detect your carrots.

## When to Sow

Early spring through to midsummer, depending on the variety.

Straight from the ground to the table—freshly pulled carrots retain all of their crunch, flavor, and nutrients.

## When to Harvest

Start harvesting as soon as they are large enough to be useful. Remove small carrots along the row, leaving those remaining more room to grow. Covered in a mulch of straw or a layer of fleece carrots can be left in the ground through reasonably cold winters and harvested as needed.

## How Many?

6 ½–10 ft. (2–3 m) rows every three or four weeks until mid- to late summer.

## Repeat Sowing

To keep up a supply of carrots you need to keep sowing them from early spring to mid- to late summer every three weeks (about five or six batches). The final sowing should be a variety that will last well in the ground in milder areas until needed in autumn or winter, or that stores well, such as 'Autumn King 2.'

## Ideal Conditions

This is the one area in which carrots are a bit fussy. Carrots do best in warm, dryish ground, and carrots in dry ground should be sweeter. To form perfect, long taproots carrots need to swell without constraints, so stony, heavy soils may produce stunted or misshapen roots. There are two ways to tackle this problem: the easiest and least time consuming is to grow short rooted or globe varieties that won't be affected by the heavy soil. The other requires more work in modifying your soil to suit the carrots; if you prize long, slender-rooted varieties, then work some sharp sand into the bed just before planting. If you are working in raised beds you should have already escaped these difficulties.

Sowing carrots into a bed that has been recently mulched with compost or manure results in "forking" or "fanging," meaning that the roots twist and become deformed, forming two or three taproots instead of one. A few years ago, left with no alternative, I sowed carrots in a recently mulched bed, which resulted in a high proportion of forked, amusingly shaped carrots that were popular with the children! Many were unaffected and, although the comical carrots were hard to prepare, they tasted fine. So if you are left with this situation, it is not a complete disaster!

## Maintenance

Carrots won't grow well with competition from weeds, so hoe regularly. Carrots arranged in neat, straight rows makes hoeing much easier.

## When to Water

In very dry spells thoroughly drench every two weeks. Heavy rain or watering after a dry spell can cause the roots to split.

## Common Problems and Solutions

**Carrot fly** is probably the biggest potential threat to your carrot crop. This is a small fly that is attracted to growing carrots by smell. They lay eggs in the soil near the top of the carrots and the maggots burrow into the soil and into the tasty taproot, leaving a mess of fine tunnels. To protect your crop from carrot fly sow seed thinly and never thin out the seedlings. The scent generated by thinning out will really draw in the carrot fly. A physical barrier of fine insect barrier mesh will prevent them getting to the carrots, as will a vertically strung fence of mesh around the bed around 20 in. (50 cm) high—carrot fly are not strong flyers and cannot fly over this. However, this type of protection can become an obstruction to gardening and is time consuming to erect and remove for harvesting, so I have experimented with keeping things simple. Every time I sow a row of carrots I sow a row of spring onions of equal length in the center of the gap between rows, or I plant my carrots between rows of garlic and onions. So far this has proved incredibly effective and resulted in perfect carrots every time. However, if you are in a badly affected area and a physical barrier doesn't appeal, you could try one of the resistant varieties, like 'Maestro,' although the resistance is only partial.

**Bolting** may be a problem in extreme drought. Remove the bolting plant immediately as it may give off hormones encouraging others to bolt, too.

◄ The best way to retain all of the healthy nutrients when cooking carrots is to boil them whole.

# Radishes ★ ★ ✰

The radish is the ultimate catch crop. It is not worth planning where to grow it as it can be slotted in among other slow-growing crops, such as cabbages, and will be ready to harvest while they are still in their infancy—a sensible way to make the best use of your growing space. Radishes are easy to grow and will obligingly produce their tasty roots with little attention from you. A good, crisp radish adds a peppery note and splash of color to summer salads.

◀ 'French Breakfast' radishes are crisp, mild, and best eaten when young.

## Varieties to Try
**'French Breakfast 3'** has elongated, cylindrical roots with a white tip and a mild flavor.
**'Cherry Belle'** has good, crisp flesh and, as you might expect, is round and red like a cherry. This is an early variety.
**'Il Candela Di Fuoco'** is an Italian radish that produces long, tapered roots a bit like a carrot. Red-skinned with white crisp flesh, they are amazingly quick to mature.

## Plant or Seed?
Seed.

## Spacing and Planting
Direct sow thinly in furrows ⅜ in. (1 cm) deep and 6 in. (15 cm) apart. Squeeze rows in along the edges of beds, in between other crops, or wherever there is a small space. The seed can be broadcast.

## When to Sow
Sow from early spring to early autumn.

## When to Harvest
Probably within four weeks of sowing, three if conditions are good. As soon as the roots are large enough for the table, pull at intervals along the row so others can fill out.

## How Many?
One row a yard (meter) or two long every two to three weeks should be ample. Better to plant a few and harvest them while young and crisp, as old radishes get woody and pithy and are not good to eat.

## Repeat Sowing
If you want a continuous supply, sow every two to three weeks.

## Ideal Conditions
Good, rich, well-drained soil.

## Maintenance
If sown too thickly they can be thinned once the seedlings are large enough, but it is easier to sow thinly and leave them to jostle for space.

## When to Water
Too much water will give all top and no bottom with lush leaves and no tasty root, so limit watering to once a week in dry spells.

## Common Problems and Solutions
**Flea beetle** is one of the few problems affecting radishes; they pepper the leaves with tiny holes. Established plants will survive and as it is only the root you are after it is not a problem. Small seedlings, however, could be killed. Draping a piece of horticultural fleece over the plants will easily thwart flea beetle.

The fabulous color and peppery taste of radishes make repeat sowing throughout the summer worthwhile.

'Boltardy' is the most reliable beet (beetroot) I've grown, but this doesn't mean compromising on taste as its flesh is sweet and smooth.

# Beets (Beetroot) ★ ★ ✣

This is a fantastically easy root vegetable, and not only do you get delicious roots that can be boiled, roasted, or enjoyed cold in salads, but also the young leaves taste great, too. Unlike other root crops, beets (beetroot) will be quite happy if your soil is a little on the thin side, as long as it doesn't dry out. Homegrown beets (beetroot) harvested when small (about the size of a squash ball) have a wonderfully sweet, earthy flavor too good to drown in malt vinegar! Preparation can be a little messy but is much easier if you cook the beets (beetroot) first, then peel them, and always twist the leaves off to limit "bleeding." Growing your own gives you the chance to experiment with yellow and white varieties seldom available in the stores. Great beginner's crop.

The flesh of the beets (beetroot) should be tender and most are best enjoyed before they get too large and become woody.

### Varieties to Try
**'Boltardy'** reliably produces sumptuously colored spherical roots. It has the advantage of being resistant to bolting and can be sown earlier than any other variety. **'Burpee's Golden'** is a fantastic beet (beetroot); its flesh is a remarkable sunshine gold color that is little diminished by cooking.

### Plant or Seed?
Plug plants are less work. Direct sowing works well as the seeds are in clusters and easy to handle, but they have to be soaked overnight before sowing.

### Spacing and Planting
Leave 3 ¼ in. (8 cm) between clusters of plants. Each plug of compost will have a cluster of small plants—don't separate them; plant them as they are and leave the roots to develop as a cluster.

### When to Plant
Mid-spring to midsummer. Young plants need protecting from frost, so just fling a length of horticultural fleece over them if cold weather is forecast.

### When to Harvest
Start harvesting when the roots are large enough to use.

### Repeat Sowing
If you buy plugs you could start harvesting small, taking roots at intervals along the row and leaving others to grow on, but accept that by mid- to late summer your beets (beetroot) will be finished. The alternative is to grow from seed and sow every three or four weeks until midsummer—it depends how much you love beets (beetroot). You could split the difference by planting a batch of plugs in mid-spring and then a row of seeds about four weeks later if you have space.

### Ideal Conditions
Beets (beetroot) thrive in a well-drained, moist soil and an open, sunny bed.

### Maintenance
Add a thick layer of mulch between the rows every couple of weeks. On one occasion I mulched one row of beets (beetroot) and the second got forgotten. The crop in the mulched row performed far better.

### When to Water
Beets (beetroot) really do need regular watering to prevent the soil drying out, because if the soil dries out they will bolt. A good soaking every couple of weeks should do the trick.

### Common Problems and Solutions
**Bolting** (producing flower heads) is the most common problem with beets (beetroot). They will bolt if planted too early and if the soil is too cold or if the soil dries out. Planting when the soil has warmed a little in mid-spring and keeping the plants well watered should prevent bolting. The best defense is to grow the popular cultivar 'Boltardy,' which is resistant to bolting and can be planted earlier than any other beets (beetroot).

# Jerusalem Artichokes ✦ ✦ ✦

Even simpler to grow than potatoes, Jerusalem artichokes are often forgotten but well worth growing. They form tubers under the ground like potatoes but have top growth that can grow between 5 ft. (1.5 m) and 10 ft. (3 m) tall with sunflower-like blooms. They will grow just about anywhere, even in partial shade, and are harvested in the lean period in the kitchen garden. They are versatile, too—they can be boiled, baked, and roasted or used to make a thick, warming winter soup. They do take up a fair amount of space and the height of their top growth can cast a shadow over other beds, but the yield you get for the virtually zero attention earns them a place if you have a large plot. They can also be grown as a windbreak.

## Varieties to Try
'Fuseau' has smooth-skinned tubers that are much easier to prepare than the more knobby cultivars.

## Plant or Seed?
Tubers.

## Spacing and Planting
Plant the tubers 4–6 in. (10–15 cm) deep in rows 12 in. (30 cm) apart.

## When to Plant
Plant tubers in early spring.

## When to Harvest
Start harvesting in early winter and dig them as you need them. Make sure you remove every tuber, not only because it is a shame to miss out on any of your harvest, but also because any tubers left will grow in the following year, probably most inconveniently in the midst of another crop. Some people treat them as a perennial in the garden and save time and expense by deliberately leaving a tuber or so from each plant.

## How Many?
Each tuber you plant should yield about eight to ten more.

## Repeat Sowing
No.

## Ideal Conditions
Jerusalem artichokes are wonderfully undemanding and will grow in most soils and even in slight shade.

## Maintenance
Earthing up the plants when they are about 12 in. (30 cm) tall can help keep the plants stable. Some gardeners advise cutting back growth to about 5 ft. (1.5 m) tall in midsummer to concentrate the plant's resources on producing tubers, but it doesn't seem to be necessary. Cut back stems in the autumn when they begin to go yellow; leave about 12 in. (30 cm) of stalk so you know where they are. Leave the cut stems on the soil to protect the tubers from frost.

## When to Water
In prolonged dry periods.

## Common Problems and Solutions
**Slugs** are probably the most likely problem, nibbling into the tubers underground. It is impossible to protect them, so use the general strategies for keeping slugs under control outlined on page 185.

Tubers of Jerusalem Artichoke 'Fuseau' are smoother than most varieties and so are much easier to prepare.

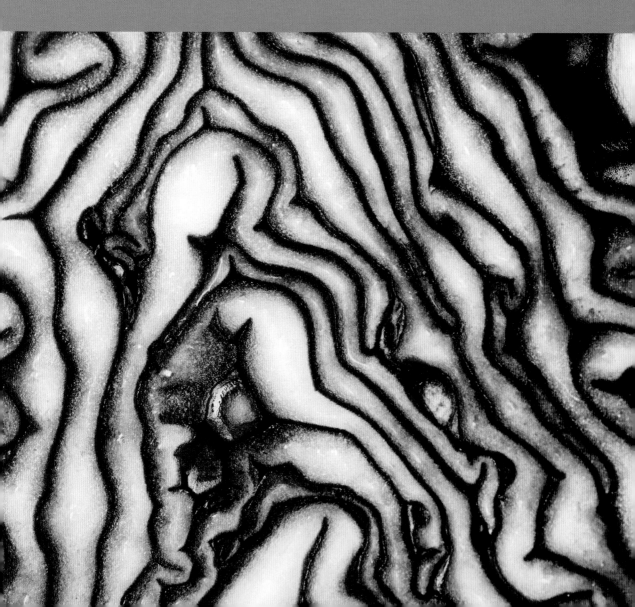

# Brassicas

**Cabbage • Broccoli and Calabrese • Kale**

# Cabbage ★ ✧ ✧

There are many varieties of cabbage that occupy growing space and mature at different times of the year. It can be hard to find room for them through the summer when the garden is full to the point of bursting, but cultivars planted in late summer or early autumn that produce crisp, sweet spring cabbages when little else is ready are very worthwhile growing. If you are a cabbage fanatic, however, you could have homegrown cabbage throughout the year—the hardiest varieties will tolerate temperature to around 14ºF (-10ºC). I grow just a few summer cabbages, mostly red varieties, because I would rather devote the space to other crops and also because growing them later in the season means that caterpillars are not a problem. However, cabbages are not the easiest veg to grow.

▶ Winter savoy-type cabbages such as 'Tundra' form tightly packed heads of pale, crinkled leaves.

## Varieties to Try
### SPRING

'**Spring Hero**' produces a large, crisp, round head that will stand well.

### SUMMER

'**Kilaxy**' is a great variety for gardens with a clubroot problem as it has good resistance. It produces a firm, round head ready in late summer that will stand into the autumn.
'**Hispi**' is a pointed cultivar that is very fast-growing and versatile.
'**Red Jewel**' is a very fast-growing red cabbage that delivers early sweet, dense hearts that will stand well.

### WINTER

'**Tundra**' is the hardiest of all. Perfect for cold areas, this extremely crinkled savoy-type cabbage will stand through very hard winters. The only snag is each cabbage will have occupied about 18 square in. (45 square cm) of your plot for probably seven or eight months, several of them being prime growing time.

### Plant or Seed?
Plants. You will only need a few plants, so it makes sense to buy just the right number.

### Spacing and Planting
The spacing of cabbage plants will directly affect the size of the head each plant produces. If a greater quantity of smaller cabbages would suit your needs, then plant closer together. Spring and summer cabbages should be planted about 12 in. (30 cm) apart. Winter varieties need more space, about 16–18 in. (40–45 cm) apart. Cabbages have a shallow root system, so they need firm soil, planted a little more deeply than they were originally grown, and to be firmed in well when they are planted. Firm the roots in with your heel—it seems brutal for such small plants, but it pays!

### When to Plant
Spring cabbages in late summer.
Summer cabbages in early to mid-spring.
Winter cabbages in late spring.

## When to Harvest

Spring cabbages will be ready to harvest the following spring and they can be used as spring greens before the hearts form. Summer cabbages are fast-growing and are ready from midsummer, but they are not hardy and should be harvested before winter. Winter varieties are slow-growing and do not mature until late autumn or winter, and they should stand through the winter.

## How Many?

Ten to twelve of any season's cabbage will probably be ample, but it is a simple crop to calculate.

## Repeat Sowing

A supply at different times of year is ensured by planting different varieties.

## Ideal Conditions

All cabbages will do best in rich soil with plenty of organic matter. They much prefer alkaline conditions, so if you have an acid soil, lime the soil before planting.

## Maintenance

Protect from pests and keep the weeds down. I mulch around spring varieties early in the year when I mulch the whole garden to give them a boost. They can be mulched with paper or grass cuttings at any time to suppress weeds.

## Growing Cabbages

1. Plant young cabbage plants a little more deeply than they were in the containers and firm them in well.

2. Fit a collar of cardboard, carpet, or a purpose-made collar from a garden center around the plant stem to prevent damage from cabbage root fly.

## When to Water

Water young plants regularly until they are established, as well as in dry periods. Spring cabbages need little watering as they grow through the colder and wetter months of the year, but summer cabbages need a regular watering to achieve lots of leaves and a good heart.

## Common Problems and Solutions

**Caterpillars and birds** are likely to be the biggest threat to cabbages, as with any brassica crop. They can be protected with mesh or chicken wire cloches (see pages 186–187).

**Clubroot** is a fungal disease that distorts the root system of brassicas, limiting their growth and causing leaves to wilt and turn brown. If you suspect clubroot is a problem, dig up a plant and take a look at the roots. Unfortunately, if it is clubroot all the plants have to be lifted and destroyed. Leave it as long as possible before planting any brassicas in that spot, as once it is in the soil clubroot persists for perhaps 20 years, far longer than any rotation system. Liming the soil can help, along with choosing a good clubroot-resistant variety, such as 'Kilaxy.'

**Cabbage root fly** lays its eggs at soil level by the stem of the cabbage plant and the larvae hatch and feed on the roots of the plants. A small disk of cardboard, carpet, or a purpose-made collar from the garden center fitted closely around the stem of the plant can prevent the cabbage root fly getting near the stem.

3. Add a covering of fine mesh or a homemade chicken wire cloche to prevent butterflies laying their eggs on the cabbages and hungry caterpillars ravaging your crop.

4. Plant a fast-growing crop between slow-to-mature cabbages to use the space efficiently. Here beets (beetroot) (to be harvested as baby beets) are being grown in the gaps, but radishes and spring onions would also work well.

# Broccoli and Calabrese ★ ✵ ✵

These plants are similar and often confused. Calabrese is often sold as broccoli in supermarkets but the difference is that broccoli, or more accurately sprouting broccoli, essentially produces through the winter in milder climates and produces a number of edible shoots, although there are faster-maturing new varieties such as 'Bordeaux' that could produce in as little as 10–15 weeks from planting. Calabrese produces a single central head, and will produce side shoots once this is harvested, and matures in the summer. They are both sown at a similar time, but the sprouting broccoli occupies the ground for longer, is a much larger plant, and will therefore probably need staking. It is, however, easier to grow than calabrese. Both produce flower heads that have to be picked before they open. The homegrown taste is unmistakable but after years of experimenting I give my space to the much more straightforward to grow kale.

### Varieties to Try
Calabrese '**Trixie**' is a compact plant that is resistant to clubroot.
Calabrese '**Iron Man**' is a resilient variety, ready to harvest from midsummer. Resistant to crown rot, *Fusarium*, and downy mildew, plus it stands well in the garden.
Sprouting broccoli '**Claret**' has a very attractive dark red color.
Sprouting broccoli '**Bordeaux**' is a very early broccoli, producing sprouts from late summer through to autumn.

### Plant or Seed?
Plants.

### Spacing and Planting
About 12 in. (30 cm) between plants. If you have an acid soil, lime it before planting. Use a collar to prevent cabbage root fly.

### When to Plant
Both broccoli and calabrese can be transplanted outside in mid-to late spring.

### When to Harvest
Calabrese should be ready to harvest from mid- to late summer, while sprouting broccoli is harvested in the winter months.

### How Many?
Ten to twelve plants should give a worthwhile yield.

### Repeat Sowing
No.

### Ideal Conditions
Very rich, fertile soil with plenty of organic matter—the nitrogen levels in the previous season's legume bed can give all brassica crops a boost.

### Maintenance
Broccoli will need staking through the winter—the plants can reach 3 ft. (1 m) high and have relatively shallow roots. Protect from pests and diseases.

### When to Water
Water transplants until they are established, but avoid over-watering broccoli as its growth has to be tough enough to make it through the winter, and fleshy growth may rot. Calabrese needs to be kept moist throughout the growing season.

### Common Problems and Solutions
Same as for Cabbages on page 91.

◄ This purple sprouting broccoli looks just as good in the vegetable patch as it does on the dinner table.

# Kale ★ ★ ✭

Kale is one of the hardiest winter vegetables and the easiest, least-fussy brassica to grow, delivering a multitude of dark crinkled leaves through the leanest time in the veg patch. It is versatile, too, and some varieties can be used as cut-and-come-again salad leaves. The craggy plants are in fact quite ornamental, especially when ennobled by sparkling frost. After much trial and error I think kale and spring cabbages seem to be the brassicas to which it is most worthwhile devoting space. I find kale so much more straightforward than other brassicas that produce in milder climates through the winter, such as broccoli and Brussels sprouts, as it produces for months in return for the absolute minimum of care and it is more popular and versatile.

## Varieties to Try

**'Black Tuscany'** or **'Cavolo Nero'** has narrow dark leaves. It looks good, tastes great, and better still can be grown as a cut-and-come-again salad crop. As it is an upright variety it takes up less space than others. **'Redbor'** is a colorful, frilly kale that is very decorative and has a strong flavor. It is very hardy and has good resistance to pests and diseases.

## Plant or Seed?

Either—I have had success with both. Seed sown directly into the ground has always germinated reliably and grown easily. I sow 'Black Tuscany' very thinly, and rather than thinning small plants, I let them grow to a useful size and use them in salads or stir-fries.

## Spacing and Planting

Plants you intend to harvest over winter need to be between 12 in. (30 cm) and 24 in. (60 cm) apart depending on the variety.

## When to Plant

Seeds in spring and plants in summer.

## When to Harvest

You can take some young leaves for salads and stir-fries, but the main period of harvest is late autumn and winter. Pick a few leaves from each plant each time. The seemingly spent plants should produce another batch of tender leaves in the spring before running to seed.

## How Many?

Ten to fifteen plants will deliver a good harvest.

## Repeat Sowing

No.

## Ideal Conditions

Most brassicas prefer a good, rich soil, and while kale will grow in poorer conditions, it will do better in soil with plenty of organic matter.

## Maintenance

There is really nothing to be done except keeping the weeds down by hoeing or mulching and protecting the kale from marauding pests.

## When to Water

Once the plants are established, water only in prolonged periods of very dry weather. Too much water could potentially make growth too soft to withstand the rigors of winter.

## Common Problems and Solutions

To keep the **caterpillars** of cabbage white butterflies from ravaging the leaves, **flea beetle** from eating additional tiny holes, and **pigeons** having a feast, too, the kale needs to be protected with fleece or fine mesh. Mesh is probably the best in the heat of summer as fleece can raise the temperature and humidity.

▶ Butterflies either can't or won't lay their eggs on the intricately frilly leaves of 'Redbor' kale, which saves the effort of trying to keep them off.

# Stems and Bulbs

**Asparagus • Rhubarb • Celeriac**

# Asparagus ★ ★ ✮

The slim shoots of crisp, young asparagus are a gourmet's delight and one of the real treats of spring. As a perennial it will occupy a fair chunk of space all year round for just a few weeks of production, and you have to resist harvesting any spears in their first season; depending on the vigor of the variety you decide to grow, perhaps take only a few in the second. So asparagus requires space, patience, and a really good start; clearing out all perennial weeds is essential along with good, rich soil. All that said, once a bed is up and running it should provide amazing asparagus for 10 to 20 years in return for being kept weed-free and covered with a good layer of mulch in the spring. So there is a fair bit of work to getting asparagus established, but if you get this right it should be plain sailing from then on. Although I love asparagus, I only added an asparagus bed to my plot after a couple of years because getting everything else right seemed a higher priority and more rewarding in the short term for less space. Ultimately, of course, I wished I had done it sooner.

▲ You don't need an asparagus steamer to enjoy this seasonal treat. I simply drizzle the spears with olive oil and roast in a low oven for 15–20 minutes.

## Varieties to Try
**'Pacific 2000'** is sweet tasting and provides a bumper harvest. This mid-season, green variety is a reliable choice.
**'Stewarts Purple'** is a new variety that is much sweeter than green cultivars. The purple color makes the spears even more appealing and it even keeps its color when lightly cooked.

## Plant or Seed?
Buy one-year-old crowns as these are the root system of an asparagus plant.

## Spacing and Planting
It is best to have a dedicated asparagus bed built for the purpose if you can. The crowns need to be about 12 in. (30 cm) apart and they can be arranged in a staggered double row. If you have more than one row, leave 18 in. (45 cm) between double rows. Soak the crowns in water for about an hour before planting.

## When to Plant
Early spring.

## When to Harvest
You should be able to take a light harvest in the spring of the following year after planting. Cut the spears about ¾ in. (2 cm) below soil level with a knife when they are about 6 in. (15 cm) tall. Once plants are established you can keep taking spears for about six weeks, then leave the spears to develop into tall, feathery ferns, allowing the plants to regenerate.

## How Many?
Twelve crowns should keep a family going. Each crown should produce about 10–12 spears in the harvest period. This will occupy about a 13 ft. (4 m) row or a 3 x 6 ½ ft. (1 x 2 m) bed.

## Repeat Sowing
To extend the harvest, plant two varieties, an early and a mid-season.

## Ideal Conditions
Asparagus needs a well-drained soil to flourish—there is no point sticking it in heavy soil and hoping for the best. If you are working in flat beds in heavy soil, building a raised bed is the best solution. It also needs plenty

of organic matter in the soil. Late frosts can also be a problem as the spears are tender.

## Maintenance

Mulch once a year in the spring. The ferny top growth may need supporting to keep it from breaking in the wind and just to keep it tidy! When the foliage begins to die in the autumn, cut it down to just above soil level and put it on the compost heap.

## When to Water

In the first year keep the crowns well watered in dry conditions.

## Common Problems and Solutions

**Slugs** can damage the emerging spears—if they are a severe problem, you could consider mulching the bed with sharp grit.

**Weak and spindly spears** can be caused by a number of factors, such as picking too heavily, too soon, or for too long, or a lack of nutrients in the soil.

**Asparagus beetle** is a common pest. It is easy to spot as it boasts black and yellow stripes and its caterpillar is grayish. Both can be removed by hand along with the clumps of black eggs. If asparagus beetle is a problem, destroy the foliage at the end of the season rather than composting it.

## Planting Asparagus

1. To plant the crowns, dig a trench about 8 in. (20 cm) deep and just wide enough for the crowns. Put a layer of garden compost in the bottom, then build up a ridge of soil along the trench to sit the crowns on so that the buds will be at soil level.

2. Arrange the crowns 12 in. (30 cm) apart and spread the roots out down the sides of the ridge.

3. When all of the crowns are in position, backfill the trench with soil and mulch the whole bed with a layer of garden compost.

# Rhubarb ★ ★ ★

This is one of the vegetable garden "firsts" that I really look forward to. All the firsts are an event but some are special, such as first potatoes and first raspberries. The first rhubarb is probably the most eagerly awaited, not only because I adore a good rhubarb crumble, but also because it comes so early in the year, especially if it's forced. The other element of this miracle is that, in return for a good layer of mulch thrown around the plants once a year, I get a hefty harvest of shining, tender pink and red stems, year after year. If you like rhubarb, then you really should grow it because it's as close to no work as it gets.

▶ A well-fed rhubarb plant should yield a delicious crop of stems for about ten years.

## Varieties to Try
**'Timperley Early'** is one of the earliest varieties. It is good for forcing and its stems remain tender until late in the season.
**'Red Champagne'** is a mid-season variety that delivers a hefty crop of rich red stems.

## Plant or Seed?
Bare-root crowns or potted plants.

## Spacing and Planting
Allow each plant about 11 square feet (1 square meter) and ensure there is plenty of organic matter in the soil.

## When to Plant
Rhubarb is usually planted as dormant crowns in autumn or late winter. Pot-grown plants are available in garden centers later in the year if you miss the dormant period.

## When to Harvest
Stalks cannot be pulled from newly planted crowns. The plants need the first year to get established. In the second year forced plants can be ready from late winter to very early spring. You can keep harvesting until mid- to late summer. Never completely strip a plant—always leave about half the stems each time to allow the plant to regenerate. Stop harvesting around midsummer so the crown can recover; by this time there are plenty of other things ready for harvest and the stalks become coarser and less tasty.

The stems should always be pulled by holding the stem close to the base and pulling away from the crown while twisting slightly. Try not to dislodge forming stems. This sounds much harder than it is!

## How Many?
Two or three crowns provide enough rhubarb for most families.

## Repeat Sowing
No, but some cultivars produce slightly earlier than others.

## Ideal Conditions
Rhubarb is not difficult so long as there is plenty of organic matter in the soil.

## Maintenance
Mulch well as part of the annual mulch with well-rotted manure if you can, as this really gives the plants a boost. If none is available use garden compost.

For a really early crop, rhubarb can be forced—this means covering the crown with a large up-turned

garbage pail, chimney pot, or purpose-made terracotta forcing jar. The forcer can be stuffed with straw and put in position in late winter. The forced stems are pale, tender, and delicate and can be harvested weeks earlier than they would be otherwise. Forced plants should be given the rest of the season to recover, and the same plant should not be forced two years running.

If the crown produces a flower spike (this will look very different to the leaf stems), remove it as close to the base as possible. Established plants will survive a few weeds until they can be dealt with.

## When to Water
Only once established in extended periods of dry weather.

## Common Problems and Solutions
There is very little to worry about with rhubarb, except that old plants will gradually lose their vigor and should be replaced with new ones in a different location.

# Celeriac ✦ ✦ ✧

It seems you either love the pungent combination of celery and fennel flavors of celeriac, or you hate it. The ugly-looking swollen root has earned a place in my heart and my veg patch every year because it is so very easy to grow, and is ready to eat at a lean time. It is terrific used raw in salads, makes a good mash, works well in hearty winter soups and casseroles, and even roasts beautifully. The only down side is the length of time it is in the ground, from late spring (when planted as a plug) through the autumn and winter, but for me it really earns its space.

◄ Not the most beautiful of vegetables but one of the easiest to grow in the low-maintenance vegetable garden, as long as you have enough space.

▶ In all except the coldest areas, celeriac can be left in the ground until needed. A useful vegetable to fill the lean winter period.

## Varieties to Try
'Brilliant' produces less knobbly roots than other varieties and these don't seem to become pithy. Its flesh does not discolor.

## Plant or Seed?
Plants. Seed germination is sometimes erratic.

## Spacing and Planting
About 12 in. (30 cm) apart each way.

## When to Plant
Mid- to late spring.

## When to Harvest
You probably won't need to harvest celeriac until mid-autumn. There is so much else on offer in the garden, the roots will happily stay in the ground all winter in mild areas, or they can be protected from heavy frosts with a mulch of straw or dug and stored in a cool place. They should keep for months.

## How Many?
Twelve plants should take most people through the winter, that's one a week for twelve weeks, taking just over 11 square feet (1 square meter) of space. If you are fan and have the space, indulge yourself with more.

## Repeat Sowing
No.

## Ideal Conditions
Good, rich soil will make for good-sized roots.

## Maintenance
To help retain moisture and thwart weeds, mulch with garden compost or straw between the plants. Removing the lower leaves will encourage the roots to swell, although I often have not had time to do this and the results have been fine.

## When to Water
A good deluge once a fortnight if the weather is dry.

## Common Problems and Solutions
It would be extremely rare to have a problem with this generous and forgiving crop.

# Fruiting Vegetables

**Tomatoes • Peppers and Chillies • Eggplants (Aubergines)
Zucchinis (Courgettes) and Summer Squash (Marrows)
Pumpkins and Winter Squashes • Artichokes • Cucumbers • Sweet Corn**

# Tomatoes ★ ✦ ✦

The smell of a homegrown tomato is one of the most evocative for me and an essential part of summer—just brushing the foliage releases a burst of fragrance. As the low-maintenance vegetable garden doesn't extend to managing a greenhouse, gardeners in a cold climate will struggle to grow good tomatoes outdoors. However, in regions with enough sun there are varieties that can be grown successfully. These fall into two categories: cordon (tall) and bush tomatoes. Cordon tomatoes require a lot of time spent staking, tying-in, and pinching out the side shoots. They are generally much more demanding and exacting than bush varieties which need none of these ministrations. For this reason I stick to growing less demanding bush varieties as these produce masses of smaller fruit on low plants and demand much less time. As a rule the larger the fruit, the more sun they will need to ripen.

▶ 'Tumbler' produces a profusion of sweet bite-sized cherry tomatoes, which are always popular with children.

## Varieties to Try
'**Tumbler**' is a trailing bush variety that produces lots of succulent cherry tomatoes. Plant them near the corners of raised beds so the plants can trail over the side. They will also grow well in pots and hanging baskets, although they need a little extra care.
'**Tumbling Tom Yellow**' is a very compact plant, and this and its fellow 'Tumbling Tom Red' produce a good crop of cherry-sized tomatoes, the yellow being a little less sweet than the red.
'**Red Alert**' is an earlier equally fruitful variety.

## Plant or Seed?
Plants.

## Spacing and Planting
Leave about 18 in. (45 cm) between bush plants.

## When to Plant
After the last frost.

## When to Harvest
Pick the fruits as they ripen.

## How Many?
Three or four plants.

## Repeat Sowing
No.

## Ideal Conditions
Tomatoes do best in a warm, sunny, and sheltered spot in good soil with plenty of organic matter.

## Maintenance
Bush tomatoes are very easy to grow—all they require is a liquid feed with a high potash organic fertilizer once a week once they are flowering. If your soil is good, getting a little slipshod with the feeding doesn't seem to do too much harm.

Plant young tomato plants at the same level they were in their pots. If the weather is cold, protect them with a layer of fleece.

Trailing plants such as 'Tumbler' and 'Tumbling Tom' can be planted so that they spill out over the edge of raised beds.

## When to Water

Young plants need regular watering until they are established, then two or three times a week when the plants are in flower and the fruits are forming. There is a tendency to water tomato plants a great deal, and while this certainly swells the fruit, too much water can dilute the delicious flavor of the ripe fruits, robbing them of their sweetness.

## Common Problems and Solutions

Fortunately tomatoes grown outdoors suffer from far fewer problems than those grown under glass.
**Blight** is the most likely problem with outdoor tomatoes. This is the same disease that afflicts potatoes, and it is most likely to be a problem in cool, wet summers. Plants develop brown patches on the leaves and discolored patches on the fruits. There is little that can be done once a plant is badly affected, and the fruit and foliage have to

be removed and destroyed. There are some cultivars that show resistance to blight, such as 'Fantasio,' which are worth trying if blight is a recurrent problem in your area. **Blossom end rot** is a black patch at the base of the fruit; this is a symptom of erratic watering. It is fortunately uncommon in plants grown in the ground.

In a cool or short summer you may be left with a great number of green fruits, and you can help the last few fruits to ripen by removing some of the foliage to let more light get to the fruits. If this fails, green tomatoes can be put in a brown paper bag with a banana in a cool place to ripen. Alternatively, pickle them or make chutney! Plant marigolds among the plants to deter insect pests.

It is reassuring to know that your homegrown tomato is packed with vitamin C and antioxidants as well as flavor.

# Peppers and Chillies ★ ✳ ✳

If you are growing in a cool climate and aiming for the best harvest possible from your plot, peppers are probably not for you. A good outdoor harvest really does need Mediterranean conditions, and even if you go to a great deal of trouble and fuss with cloches the yield will probably not be good. Chillies, however, are a different matter as they are more tolerant of changes in temperature, although they too need a warm spot, and just one or two good-sized plants could deliver all the chillies you will need for the year. They are easily dried once ripe and will last if kept in a cool, dry place. In some places chillies are sometimes called chili peppers or hot peppers, creating some labeling confusion. Regardless, peppers, chillies, chili peppers, and hot peppers are essentially grown in the same manner.

## Varieties to Try
**'Apache'** is a compact variety of chilli with medium strength and plump, round-ended fruits. Can be grown in pots.
**'Bell Boy'** is a popular variety of pepper, ripening to give red fruit.
**'Big Banana'** is an unusual pepper cultivar with long, tapered fruit.

## Plant or Seed?
Plants.

## Spacing and Planting
Allow about 18 in. (45 cm) between plants.

## When to Plant
Early summer if the weather is warm.

## When to Harvest
Peppers can be harvested green or left to ripen to orange, red, or black depending on the cultivar. If you leave the peppers to ripen, then the harvest will be smaller as the plants will stop producing new fruits. Take care when harvesting chillies; wear gloves, snip them from the plant, and avoid any juice making contact with your skin.

## How Many?
One or two plants for chillies, five or six for peppers.

## Repeat Sowing
No.

## Ideal Conditions
Good, rich soil in a very warm, sheltered, sunny spot.

## Maintenance
There is little to do except feed once every couple of weeks with tomato food once in flower. If you decide to grow peppers in a cool climate, protect them with polycarbonate cloches in cool weather. At the end of the growing season snip all chillies from the plant and lay them out to dry. You can move the plant to a frost-free spot and let the chillies dry on the plant. Store the dried chillies in an airtight container.

## When to Water
Water very sparingly, especially if the weather is cool.

## Common Problems and Solutions
If the weather is cold and cloudy the fruits may fail to develop. **Aphids** (greenfly) are a common problem and can weaken young plants. They can be removed by hand, but mature plants should withstand a minor infestation. Companion planting (see page 188) may help.

◀ Chillies are a fantastic way to spice up food. For a milder effect, remove the seeds before cooking. Always take care not to touch your face or eyes when preparing chillies.

# Eggplants (Aubergines) ★ ✰ ✰

These are even more of a struggle to grow outdoors in a temperate climate than peppers. They are tropical in origin and so require sustained heat to flourish, but if you have this then they are fairly straightforward to grow. Unless you garden in a reliably warm spot, the harvest is probably not going to justify the work you have to put in to grow them outside. I have tried and the plants have fruited and the eggplants (aubergines) have been good to eat, but I could have been getting so much more for my time and space.

◀ The eggplant (aubergine) plant produces one of the prettiest flowers on the vegetable plot.

## Varieties to Try
'**Moneymaker**' is the most commonly available plant, producing long purple-black fruits.
'**Ova**' produces interesting white fruits.

## Plant or Seed?
Plants. Start with large, well-established plants in colder areas to give the best chance of a harvest.

## Spacing and Planting
Leave about 24 in. (60 cm) between plants.

## When to Plant
Summer.

## When to Harvest
The fruits are ready as soon as they are fully colored.

## How Many?
Each plant will probably yield three fruits, which isn't a great deal, so plan accordingly.

## Repeat Sowing
No.

## Ideal Conditions
Rich, moist soil.

## Maintenance
Feed the plants once a week with high potash organic fertilizer once flowering begins. To encourage the plants to become bushy, the growing tip can be removed once the plants are 12 in. (30 cm) tall.

## When to Water
Eggplants (aubergines) require plenty of water all through the season.

## Common Problems and Solutions
As for Tomatoes (see page 106).

▶ Eggplants (aubergines) are a relative of the tomato but are much more difficult to grow in temperate climates without protection.

# Zucchinis (Courgettes) and Summer Squash (Marrows) ✶ ✶ ✶

Given enough water and compost, zucchinis (courgettes) are effortless to grow. Homegrown zucchinis (courgettes) are usually available in such profusion that they can be picked while still young, sweet, and delicious, and are nothing like some of the pithy, oversized tasteless examples from the supermarket. They are a staple of so many dishes, yet are equally delicious sliced thinly in salads or simply stir-fried in butter. Even the magnificent yellow trumpet flowers are edible (see page 158). A really rewarding plant.

◀ The 'One Ball' is a bit of a novelty and adds color and interest to the vegetable plot.

▶ Picked young and sliced thinly, zucchinis (courgettes) are a good addition to summer salads.

## Varieties to Try
'One Ball' produces shining, round, yellow zucchinis (courgettes) with creamy, sweet flesh. 'One Ball' is a bit of a novelty but still pulls its weight, giving a good harvest and having a good shape for stuffing.
'Orelia' is another golden-colored cultivar. It has a very vigorous habit and produces an amazingly good yield of tasty zucchinis (courgettes).
'El Greco' has the advantage of producing early. It produces an open, erect plant that makes picking easy and a profusion of mid green, excellently flavored zucchinis (courgettes).
'Defender' is another reliable early green variety of zucchini (courgettes) worth trying, especially as it has some resistance to mosaic virus and downy mildew.

## Plant or Seed?
Zucchinis (courgettes) are reasonably easy when sown directly into the soil, but it is still easier to buy plants as you will only need three or four.

## Spacing and Planting
Each plant really does need some room—11 square feet (1 square meter) or just under—but for that space and very little work you will get an abundance, if not a glut, of zucchinis (courgettes). Plant the young plants with plenty of compost on a small mound and mulch around them with compost.

## When to Plant
Late spring.

## When to Harvest
Eight to ten weeks from planting. Pick the zucchinis (courgettes) when they are still young and tender at about 4–5 in. (10–12 cm) long and keep picking to ensure a continued supply. If you are a weekend gardener or seldom able to visit your plot, then picking the fruits young is a must, as in a week a small tender fruit can become oversized and old.

▲ It is almost miraculous how rapidly 'El Greco' can produce more fruits.

▶ 'One Ball' is an unusual, round summer squash (marrow) with a particularly sweet flesh.

## How Many?

Two to four plants should be ample, which will take 6 ½–10 ft. (2–3 m) of your growing space all through the summer. If you will be away from your plot for a couple of weeks, remove all the fruit and flowers—it seems harsh but this will ensure you have a crop to come home to.

## Repeat Sowing

No.

## Ideal Conditions

A plentiful supply of organic matter and water is the key to success with zucchinis (courgettes) and summer squash (marrows). From the start they need plenty of nutrition to generate those enormous, coarse leaves that provide the energy to keep the fruits coming. A space-saving tip is to try planting zucchinis (courgettes) and summer squash (marrows) on the compost heap as they will thrive in the rich, moist environment.

## Maintenance

Beyond mulching and watering there is little else to do except feeding once a week once fruiting has started. Young plants may need protecting from slugs and snails with a bottle cloche. Once the plants are established they can tolerate a little competition from weeds until these can be dealt with.

## When to Water

Water regularly, or employ an olla (see pages 36–37) to keep the soil moist.

## Common Problems and Solutions

**Mosaic virus**, or more correctly cucumber mosaic virus (CMV), appears as small yellow patches on the leaves that spread to give the mosaic pattern. The leaves then crinkle and the plants fail to thrive and produce few fruits. The plants are best removed and destroyed. The virus is common in the garden and spread by aphids or knives used for harvesting, so there is little that can be done to defend your crop or treat it once it is infected. Growing resistant varieties such as 'Defender' is the best solution.

**Powdery mildew** is less serious and usually strikes during the autumn. A white powder appears on the leaves and the plants tend to lose their vitality and production slows. Badly affected leaves can be removed and the plants can be perked up with some lavish watering and a liquid feed if you aren't doing so already.

To be grown well, pumpkins and squashes need to be left on the plant until the skin hardens, then cut leaving a long stalk and left in the sun until they sound hollow when tapped.

# Pumpkins and Winter Squashes ✦ ✦ ✦

These plants require a great deal of space. Their stems roam across the soil and throw up enormous crinkled leaves, but this prodigious growth means they are immensely satisfying to grow, and the flowers are edible, too. Fiery orange pumpkins are stunningly ornamental. A neat space-saving technique is to grow your squashes under your sweet corn as neither will interfere with the growth of the other and you get two crops from one bed. This is part of the Native American Three Sisters planting, where beans, sweet corn, and squashes were grown together to really get the most out of a small space. The squashes' large leaves also help to suppress weeds. Squashes can be trained up obelisks or other support as a space-saving strategy, but even so in a small plot large pumpkins will probably be impractical and in cooler regions they can be unreliable.

▲ Reducing the number of fruits on each plant will increase the likelihood of achieving good-sized pumpkins.

## Varieties to Try
'**Racer**' produces plenty of large, perfectly shaped Halloween pumpkins. Each year my children grow one plant each, competing for the honors of largest, most beautiful, and most abundant pumpkins.
'**Jack of All Trades**' is another great pumpkin for carving, with each plant producing plenty of large, orange fruits.
'**Cobnut**' is a variety of butternut squash that is tasty and sweet when roasted. It is a fast-maturing variety, which is helpful in cooler areas.

## Plant or Seed?
Plants.

## Spacing and Planting
As pumpkin and squash cultivars vary enormously, refer to the instructions for the particular variety you are growing.

## When to Plant
Late spring.

## When to Harvest
Early autumn.

## Repeat Sowing
No.

## Ideal Conditions
Rich, moist soil in a sunny spot.

## Maintenance
Nothing beyond regular watering. Cut away leaves at the end of the season to allow fruits to ripen and gather before first frosts.

## When to Water
Pumpkins have good root systems and so need less water than you might expect, but keep the soil moist.

## How Many?
Pumpkin and squash cultivars vary enormously in the size and shapes of the fruit they produce, so it is hard to be prescriptive. They take up plenty of space, too. If you love pumpkin and have plenty of space, try three or four plants, otherwise start with one or two.

## Common Problems and Solutions
**Powdery mildew** is a possible threat (see Zucchinis [Courgettes] and Summer Squash [Marrows] on page 114).
**Slugs and snails** can devour young plants, so protect plants with plastic bottle cloches.

# Artichokes ✦ ✦ ⚹

Pick the flower buds just before they open.

The statuesque globe artichoke has much to recommend it to the time-poor gardener. It is a perennial, and given a sunny spot should carry on producing tasty buds for four or five years with little attention. Artichokes generally start producing in early summer, which can be a lean time in the vegetable plot, and are a real gourmet treat. The down side is that each plant will permanently occupy about 11 square feet (1 square meter) of space and the yield for the space occupied is not immense. However, if you have the room and really enjoy eating them, they are easy to grow and can be treated just like any herbaceous perennial.

## Varieties to Try

'**Green Globe**' is perhaps the most commonly available variety, but not perhaps the tastiest. It produces large green buds and is reasonably hardy.
'**Purple Globe**' is hardier than 'Green Globe' and produces similarly large buds with fleshy bases to its scales.
'**Violetto di Chioggia**' is very beautiful and would be an asset in any flower border, but it may be difficult to find. It is very early, producing smaller buds with dark purple scales.

## Plant or Seed?

For a quick start, buy established plants of named cultivars in pots from the garden center or by mail order. They can be grown from seed or supplied as rooted offsets.

## Spacing and Planting

Consider that the plants will be about 5 ft. (1.5 m) tall with large, arching, silvery leaves and so likely to cast shade over neighboring beds.

## When to Plant

Late winter.

## When to Harvest

Early summer.

## How Many?

Space might be a factor. I recommend three plants.

## Repeat Sowing

Plant varieties that produce at different times, if you have space.

## Ideal Conditions

Globe artichokes thrive in a well-drained, rich soil in an open, sunny environment. Dig in some well-rotted manure when planting and on heavier, poorly drained soils add grit.

## Maintenance

A good layer of compost around the plants during the annual mulch will build up the plants and improve harvests. If they are in a windy spot provide some support—a simple cane should do—to prevent the brittle stems from breaking. At the end of the season when the leaves wither, cut back the foliage, and in frost-prone areas protect the crown with straw or horticultural fleece.

## When to Water

In prolonged periods without rainfall.

## Common Problems and Solutions

**Blackfly** is the most likely problem that congregates on the shoots and buds. The best treatment is to dislodge them with a strong jet of water before the infestation gets too great.

Technically not a fruit but a flower bud, the artichoke is probably more fuss to eat than it is to grow!

# Cucumbers ★ ✷ ✷

Homegrown outdoor cucumbers are slightly different to greenhouse varieties. They tend to be shorter and rough skinned but they taste every bit as good, and thankfully the outdoor varieties are much easier to manage than their glasshouse relatives. Cucumbers do best when grown up an obelisk or some form of support and so take up little growing space. Once they are established they produce fruits at an astonishing rate. Even outdoor varieties, however, need a warm and sheltered location to succeed. Do note that it is not worth trying indoor varieties outside as they are rarely a success.

## Varieties to Try
**'Burpless Tasty Green'** is as tasty as its name promises and has no bitterness. It has always done well for me, even in poor summers.
**'Green Fingers'** produces masses of small cucumbers with a good flavor. One cucumber is just about an individual portion, and these are very popular with children. Resistant to powdery mildew.

## Plant or Seed?
Plants.

## Spacing and Planting
Space the plants about 24 in. (60 cm) apart. Draw up the soil into a mound and plant the young plant on the top. Handle the young plants with care as they are brittle and resent the disturbance of being transplanted. Mulch around the plants.

## When to Plant
In early summer when all risk of frost has passed.

## When to Harvest
Pick fruits as they form, as soon as they fill out. Very young fruits may not be the best tasting, while very old plants will have tough skin and pronounced seeds. Always cut the cucumber from the plant as the stems are brittle and likely to break.

## How Many?
Two or three plants.

## Repeat Sowing
No.

## Ideal Conditions
Very rich, moist soil in a warm spot. Cucumbers won't do well in a cold, windy location.

## Maintenance
Thick layers of mulch will help to keep the soil warm and retain moisture. Planting through a sheet mulch of black plastic can help keep the roots warm and suppress weeds. The plants can suffer a slight check in growth after planting but should recover and grow strongly.

## When to Water
At least twice a week, copiously once growing strongly.

## Common Problems and Solutions
**Slugs** will attack young plants, so use plastic bottle cloches to protect them.
**Mildew** often coats the leaves toward the end of the summer; remove the affected leaves and destroy them and the plant should continue to produce.
**Cucumber mosaic virus** can also be a problem (see under Zucchinis [Courgettes] and Summer Squash [Marrows] on page 114).

◀ Cucumbers can be trained up any support or left to scramble through plants at ground level.

# Sweet Corn ✦ ✦ ✧

Grow the right varieties and you will never have tasted sweet corn so sweet, so tender, and so delicious. Most sweet corn varieties are now termed "supersweet" (the sweetest) or "sugar-enhanced," and they contain far more sugars than the regular varieties. The yield for the growing space they occupy is not the best, but it is reasonable, and the cobs, cooked just minutes after picking, are so unlike anything you can buy they are well worth growing. As soon as a cob is picked the sugars start turning into starch, so the supermarket will never be able to match the taste. The cobs tend to all ripen at once unless you carefully stagger repeat sowing. Cold weather can also prevent ripening and the supersweet cultivars do need warmer conditions to do well.

◀ Statuesque sweet corn plants are wonderfully decorative and don't look out of place among the flowers for cutting.

## Varieties to Try
'**Lark**' is a tendersweet variety—it is sweet like the supersweets but even more tender and easier to digest. The cobs are not large but the taste is indescribably good. '**Earlibird**' is a supersweet cultivar that produces lovely, neat cobs earlier than any other supersweet.

## Plant or Seed?
Growing from small plants is recommended, but handle them carefully as sweet corn resent root disturbance.

## Spacing and Planting
Plant 14 in. (35 cm) apart in each direction in blocks rather than rows. Sweet corn is wind-pollinated and planting in a block gives the best chance of good pollination. Position the plants so they are a little deeper than they were in the pots to encourage adventitious roots and to keep them stable. In warm areas direct sowing is possible but only when the soil temperature

has really warmed up in early summer.

Sweet corn is one of the crops that can be planted through a sheet of black plastic to cut back on the need for weeding and to keep the roots warm. Mulching well and underplanting with squashes will help to keep weeds down, too.

## When to Plant
Late spring to early summer after the risk of frost has passed.

## When to Harvest
Mid- to late summer. Once the silks or tassels on the cobs begin to turn brown the sweet corn is probably ripe. To check if sweet corn is ripe and ready for picking, carefully peel back the green outer covering and the filaments and push your nail into the kernels. If the juice is milky then the cob is ripe. Twist the ripe cob off, leaving the second to ripen.

This cob is not quite ripe, as its tassel, or silk, has not turned brown yet.

## How Many?

Sixteen plants should yield around 32 cobs, requiring a block of growing space of just over 16 square feet (1.5 square meters).

## Repeat Sowing

Possible if you have enough room and the temperatures are adequate. Often late plantings won't ripen because the autumn weather is not warm enough.

## Ideal Conditions

Sweet corn needs good soil with plenty of organic matter. If you can put them in last season's pea bed they will enjoy the nitrogen left in the soil by the peas.

## Maintenance

In windy areas earth can be piled up around the stems to keep them stable. Once established they are tall enough not to be smothered by a few weeds, but it is much smarter to cut down on weeding around sweet corn plants by applying a good mulch and planting small squashes or zucchinis (courgettes) between the plants. The two crops will grow happily together, and the mulch and the tough, spreading leaves of the squash or zucchinis (courgettes) will suppress weeds. You also get two crops out of one space.

## When to Water

Sweet corn plants need plenty of water, especially as the cobs are swelling.

## Common Problems and Solutions

**Underdeveloped cobs** or bald patches on the cobs caused by poor pollination are the most common problems with sweet corn.

**Slugs and birds** can also be a problem, and sweet corn is one of the young plants I try to plant out with a plastic bottle cloche to protect the tender leaves. The plants also enjoy the extra warmth they offer. The same bottles can be used to protect the ripening cobs from squirrels later in the season if they are a problem.

◄ Sweet corn tastes best cooked almost immediately after picking. Wrap a cob in foil and cook quickly on the grill to retain the flavor.

# Allium Family

**Onions • Shallots • Garlic • Leeks
Spring Onions**

# Onions ✦ ✦ ✦

Once planted, all a row of onions requires is occasional hoeing to keep weeds from swamping them, and that's it. Their undemanding nature and their status as a basic in the kitchen make them a natural choice for those wanting to get the maximum out of their vegetable garden with little effort. They can be planted in spring or autumn, and for those juggling crops on a small plot autumn sowing makes sense as the onions will occupy the space over the winter when there are fewer demands. As you begin to harvest them in June, zucchinis (courgettes) and summer squash (marrows) can then fill the gap, making economical use of growing space.

▶ 'Hercules' is reputed to be an excellent keeper.

## Varieties to Try
**'Red Delicious'** is a large, sweet red onion that matures early when planted in the spring.
**'Radar'** is an autumn-planting variety that has a mild flavor and a strong resistance to bolting.
**'Hercules'** produces a yellow, round-shaped bulb that keeps well and is suitable for spring planting.
**'Senshyu Yellow'** is planted in the autumn for an early harvest the following summer. The tops can be used in the same way as chives.

## Plant or Seed?
Onions are most straightforward when grown from sets—these are small, partially grown onions where the growth has been arrested, leaving them ready to spring into life once planted. Growing from seed is possible but not worthwhile for the busy gardener.

## Spacing and Planting
Plant sets by pushing them gently into the soil so they sit just below the surface. In heavy soils you may need to use a trowel to avoid damaging the set. If birds are a problem in your garden, snip off the papery tip so they can't drag the set out of the soil. If you want the biggest onions you can get, plant them 4 in. (10 cm) apart, and

if you would like a few smaller onions plant some 2 in. (5 cm) apart, cramming more into the space. Leave 8 in. (20 cm) between rows.

## When to Plant
Overwintering varieties are planted in early autumn, and main crop onions in mid- to late spring.

## When to Harvest
You can begin taking a few autumn-planted onions in early summer, while the rest of the crop can be lifted when the tops turn yellow and fall over, usually in midsummer. Gently ease each onion out of the ground and leave them in the sun or in a sheltered porch or shed to allow the skins to harden. Store them by tying them in bunches, hanging them in a net sack or making strings and hanging them in a cool, airy place.

## How Many?
Your onion yield is easy to predict—you plant 50 sets and you should get 50 onions, although the sizes may vary. Sets are often sold by weight and 50 sets weighs about 7 oz. (200 g). To grow 50 large onions takes one 16 ft. (5 m) row. Just calculate how many onions you use in a week and go from there.

The easiest way to grow onions is from sets.

Snip the tip from the set and push it into the ground so it is just visible. Use a dibble in hard ground.

### Repeat Sowing
No.

### Maintenance

Onions won't grow well if there is competition from weeds, so once every couple of weeks quickly hoe between the rows slicing young weed plants from their roots. A time-saving solution is to grow onions through a sheet mulch of black plastic.

### When to Water

Onions really don't need watering unless the weather is exceptionally dry, as they develop a deep root system and it seems regular watering has little effect on their production. In fact, too much water at the end of the growing period can be detrimental as the onions won't keep as well.

### Common Problems and Solutions

**White rot** causes onion leaves to become yellow and fluffy and white mold with black spots to form around the bulb. This is a fungal disease with fruiting bodies that can persist in the soil, infecting any member of the allium family. Unfortunately, this is one of the rare vegetable garden problems with no solution, but with care the problem can be contained and avoided in subsequent years. Any infected onions must be destroyed and not composted. Leave it as long as possible before growing onions or leeks in the affected bed as the disease can persist in the soil for up to eight years.

**Bolting** can be a problem (onions producing a flower spike)—if you come across this try growing heat-resistant varieties. These are more expensive but have a reduced instance of bolting.

**Mildew** can also be a problem, causing a white fungal growth to appear on the leaves. Affected leaves should be removed and destroyed, but the bulbs should still be usable, although they will probably not store well.

Lifted onions need to be left in the sun or a warm place to allow the skins to harden.

# Shallots ✦ ✦ ✦

As blissfully easy to grow as onions, shallots have a special flavor and sweetness, although they tend to be expensive and harder to find in stores. In most respects they are managed in the same way as onions, but each set you plant will grow into a cluster of shallots all about the same size. For each set you plant you should harvest at least five or six shallots.

◄ ► This healthy clump of 'Jermor' miraculously delivers eight shallots for the one set I planted and all I've done is hoe a few times!

## Varieties to Try
'**Jermor**' produces long, thin bulbs with a copper-colored skin, pinky flesh, and a superb flavor, and I find they keep remarkably well.
'**Delvad**' gives a good yield of round bulbs, eight to ten per cluster. It has tasty, pinkish flesh.

## Plant or Seed?
Sets. If you get the chance to choose your own, small ones are less likely to bolt.

## Spacing and Planting
They can be spaced at 6 in. (15 cm) apart with 8 in. (20 cm) between rows or 4 in. (10 cm) apart with 12 in. (30 cm) between rows. Push them into the soil so the tops are just level with the surface of the soil. As with onions, snip off the papery tip to prevent birds from unearthing the set. If you find sets on the surface, just poke them back in.

## When to Plant
Winter or early to mid-spring.

## When to Harvest
As soon as they look large enough you can start taking a few for cooking. Then when the foliage yellows and dies back, lift the clumps of shallots and leave them to dry off in the sun or in a dry, airy space. They can be stored in trays, netting sacks, or tied into bunches in a frost-free, dry place.

## How Many?
Each shallot will give a harvest of about five or six more, so 30 sets should yield about 150 shallots, which is probably plenty. It is helpful to know that 2 lb. (1 kg) of sets contain about 100 sets.

## Repeat Sowing
No.

## Ideal Conditions
Good, fertile soil.

## Maintenance
Shallots will not do well if they are competing with weeds, so hoe between the rows every couple of weeks.

## When to Water
Water in extremely dry weather.

## Common Problems and Solutions
Very trouble-free. Although they are susceptible to the same conditions as onions, they have the reputation of being more robust and problem-free.

▲ These ample cloves should produce good-sized bulbs when planted.

# Garlic ★ ★ ✭

If you regularly cook with garlic and enjoy its pungent flavors, then it should be a "must have" in your vegetable plot, not only because you can feast on wonderfully flavorsome garlic and experiment with the tastes of different varieties, but also because it is incredibly low maintenance; like most of the allium family, hoeing is the only task once they are planted until harvesting. Garlic also makes a great companion plant as its strong smell confounds pests in search of other crops. You will need to dry and store your crop but this is no hardship—they can be tied into small bundles (fancy braiding is nice but not obligatory) and kept in a dry, not-too-cool place (or it will encourage them to sprout). A good crop for beginners as long as the site is suitable.

## Varieties to Try

There are varieties suited to planting in autumn that will keep about four months from harvest, and spring-planting varieties that will keep for a couple of months longer.

'Germidour' is a mild-flavored French variety suitable for autumn planting.

'Marco' is planted in autumn and is said to keep for a year, but I can't vouch for this as mine are all eaten long before this. It has a very fine, punchy flavor.

'Cristo' produces large, strongly flavored bulbs and can be planted in autumn or spring, plus it has the advantage of a long storage period

I have read books advocating buying garlic from the supermarket to plant. I confess I have never been brave enough to try this, not wanting to risk my time, space, and garlic crop. There is a risk of viruses and nematodes infecting the crop and the variety is unknown, so it is a bit like a crapshoot where you don't know what you are growing or how long it will keep.

## Plant or Seed?

Cloves broken from a bulb of garlic. Bigger cloves produce bigger bulbs, and some of the smaller ones toward the center of the bulb may not be worth planting.

## Spacing and Planting

Leave about 6 in. (15 cm) between cloves and 12 in. (30 cm) between rows. Push them into the soil flat end first so the point is just below the surface of the soil. If you want to grow them in a block, plant the cloves 6 in. (15 cm) apart in staggered rows.

## When to Plant

Autumn or spring. I favor autumn because there are plenty of other tasks to get on with in spring.

## When to Harvest

The bulbs should be fully formed by midsummer—harvest them when the leaves fade or they may sprout new leaves. If you are impatient you can enjoy green or wet garlic sooner, whenever the bulbs look large enough.

Plant in late autumn and by early summer;
astonishingly the single clove has become a plump
bulb ready for eating.

▲ Each clove is planted flat side down with its papery tip uppermost.

▶ Break the garlic bulb into cloves. It is probably a waste of time planting very small cloves.

I roast the bulbs whole and squeeze the wonderful garlicky pulp out of the papery cases onto crusty bread.

## How Many?

Each bulb of garlic you buy should yield about ten cloves that are worth planting and each clove planted should produce a plump bulb of garlic. Three bulbs is probably a good number to begin with.

## Ideal Conditions

Garlic likes heat and well-drained soil—if you can put them in the sunniest spot. They don't need much organic matter to be added to the soil.

## Maintenance

Hoe once every couple of weeks to keep the weeds down.

## When to Water

Only in very dry spells.

## Common Problems and Solutions

**Bolting** (producing a flower spike) can be a problem, usually caused by bad weather conditions. Remove the flower spike and the bulb will still be edible (and the flower spikes are, too). Use the bulbs that bolt first.
**Rust** is a threat to all of the allium family. This is not too much of a problem, although the bulbs produced will be smaller than usual and the foliage must be destroyed rather than composted. If you have a crop blighted by rust, leave it as long as possible before growing a member of the allium family in that spot again. Rust can be a symptom of poor drainage, so it is worth investigating if you suspect there may be an underlying problem.

# Leeks ✦ ✦ ✦

The magnificent leek has many virtues: it is a cinch to grow, is ready for harvest at the leanest time in the vegetable garden, will stand through a tough winter with no extra care, its blue-green leaves look stunning through the winter, and obviously there is that very special homegrown taste. Freshly harvested leeks are crisper and juicier than the ones in the supermarket, and if you have worked organically they won't have been subjected to the wide range of sprays often used to get a commercial crop. So leeks really do earn their place in the vegetable garden. A very good crop for the novice vegetable grower.

◀ Unlike other varieties, I grow these remarkably resilient 'Atal' baby leeks from seed.

▶ The arching leaves of 'Pancho' look superb among the early autumn nasturtiums.

## Varieties to Try

**'Pancho'** is the variety I would choose if I were growing just one variety of leek, as it matures quickly but will happily stand in the bed awaiting harvest until midwinter and possibly beyond. It has a good flavor and texture.

**'Toledo'** is a good partner for 'Pancho,' as it matures later, from late autumn, and will stand through to spring. It has dark blue leaves that look majestic in the winter plot and is valuable as it is resistant to bolting.

**'Musselburgh'** is an extremely robust leek that will stand a really hard winter, so it's worth trying in really cold areas. It matures late from early winter and will stand through to spring.

**'Atal'** is a variety of baby leek I grow from seed. They don't have to be transplanted and mature in just 10 to 12 weeks to about the size of a spring onion. Useful in salads or stir-fries, they also grow well in containers.

## Plant or Seed?

Plants. Leeks are traditionally sown in a seed bed and then transplanted when they are about as thick as a pencil, but by ordering young plants you step in at the point they are transplanted. If you have the choice, as a rule, bigger transplants will produce bigger leeks.

## Spacing and Planting

Generally leeks are grown 6 in. (15 cm) apart but this can be reduced to 4 in. (10 cm) in rows 12 in. (30 cm) apart. However, if you plan on enjoying some of your crop when they are young and succulent, then you can plant some at just half that distance apart and harvest every other one while they are small, leaving the bulk of the crop to grow on to maturity.

The small leek plants are planted slightly differently to other plug plants. The leek plants may look a little droopy after planting but they will soon perk up and the holes will fill naturally with soil over time (see pages 138–139).

## When to Plant
Late spring.

## When to Harvest
You can start using a few leeks as soon as they reach a usable size (being that of the baby leeks which are sold at a premium in supermarkets), but beware of taking too many this young as you will get a lot more leek for your money later in the season. Also, in the summer there is plenty to choose from on the vegetable plot, while the leek is one of the stalwarts of the vegetable patch in winter.

## How Many?
It is simple to calculate the harvest for leeks—unless you are extremely unlucky, for each leek you plant you should pull one leek harvesting over a four- or five-month period. Fifty would be worthwhile, but 150 may not be too many for a family of leek lovers if you have the space.

## Ideal Conditions
They are really unfussy and good soil is sufficient, but they do not do well in compacted soil.

## Planting Leeks
1. Make a 6 in. (15 cm) deep hole with a dibble.

2. Drop in one leek plant, ensuring it makes it to the bottom of the hole.

## Maintenance

A truly easy crop where all there is to do is keep the weeds down with a few minutes of hoeing every week or two.

## When to Water

Only in extremely dry periods.

## Common Problems and Solutions

**Rust** is the most common problem afflicting leeks—bright, orangey brown patches that appear on the leaves. Eventually the leaves turn yellow and wilt. The best thing is to salvage what you can, cutting the leeks before the problem is too bad. Normally the white part is unaffected and can still be eaten. The rust-spotted leaves should be destroyed, not composted. If rust does strike, remember not to grow onions, leeks, garlic, or shallots on that spot for as long as possible.

3. The plants may look a little droopy after planting but don't panic as they will soon stand up.

4. Over time the holes will fill naturally with soil.

# Spring Onions ✷ ✷ ✷

Fast-growing spring or salad onions are essential, not only because they give a punchy bite to salads and stir-fries, but also because they are a great companion for carrots in the battle against carrot fly. They are quick to reach a usable size and some varieties can be left to grow on into full-sized onions, so there is no hurry or pressure to harvest the onions. There are even varieties that will stand through cold winters.

◀ Standing like soldiers, spring onions are a great way to edge an ornamental bed.

▶ Taking a few small onions as soon as they are usable creates space for those remaining to grow larger.

## Varieties to Try
'**White Lisbon Winter Hardy**' is a strong-growing variety that will stand through the winter.
'**Red Beard**' can be ready to harvest in 12 to 14 weeks and is a beautiful red color. If left in the ground they can be grown on to form bulb onions.

## Plant or Seed?
Seed.

## Spacing and Planting
Sow seed into furrows ½ in. (13 mm) deep, leaving about 6 in. (15 cm) between rows. Sprinkle the seed finely along the furrow. There is no need to thin out the onions as they will make their own space.

## When to Plant
A short row of spring onions can be slotted in anywhere around the garden but I find they are best value when planted cheek by jowl with carrots to deter carrot fly. Plant from early spring through to midsummer. Plant whenever you plant carrots.

## When to Harvest
As soon as the onion is of a usable size, or sooner if you have planted far too thickly. The tops can be used like chives.

## How Many?
A 6 ½ ft. (2 m) row every three or four weeks, or synchronize with carrots.

## Ideal Conditions
Very unfussy; reasonable soil will give a reasonable crop.

## When to Water
Water in very dry weather.

## Common Problems and Solutions
Nothing much should trouble your crop of spring onions.

# Berries and Currants

**Strawberries • Blackberries • Black, Red, and White Currants
Gooseberries • Raspberries**

# Strawberries ★ ★ ✦

Just picked and still warm from the sun, a shining, plump strawberry is one of the greatest treats in the kitchen garden. So tasty that they need to be protected from birds, which is easy, and children, which is much more difficult. Few of my strawberries make it to the table; they are consumed as a delicious al fresco snack. Growing your own means there are no compromises on flavor to achieve better shipping qualities or an excess of watering that bumps up the weight of the fruit but dilutes that glorious strawberry flavor.

▶ The sweet red fruits of the 'Florence' cultivar.

## Varieties to Try

Strawberry cultivars are so diverse in their characteristics that it is worth experimenting with a few plants of a number of varieties to find a couple of favorites you will really look forward to eating.

'**Cambridge Favorite**' ripens in mid-season and its bountiful crop of berries have a wonderfully fragrant taste.

'**Rosie**' is an exceptionally early strawberry that produces a large number of fairly small, soft fruits.

'**Florence**' is a truly prolific late variety that produces very sweet, rich red fruits. It also has good disease resistance.

'**Aromel**' is a perpetual-fruiting variety, but in reality it produces two batches of fruit. A neat trick is to grow 'Aromel' alongside a summer-fruiting variety and pick all the flowers from 'Aromel' in very early summer to ensure it gives a nice crop of berries in autumn when other cultivars are over.

'**Honeoye**' produces very dark red, flavorsome fruits early in the season.

## Plant or Seed?

Plants, bare-root or in pots.

## Spacing and Planting

Plant at 12 in. (30 cm) intervals in well-prepared soil so that the crown of the plant is just level with the surface of the soil.

## When to Plant

Autumn or spring. A strawberry bed should give a good harvest for three years. You will then need to replant in a different place.

## When to Harvest

As fruits ripen. Harvest all ripe fruit as any left will go moldy, which could spread diseases and spoil the rest of the harvest.

## How Many?

Twelve plants will give a nice amount of strawberries. In good conditions one plant can produce around 1 lb. (450 g) of strawberries.

▲ A mulch of straw under the strawberry plants keeps the fruit clean and away from the soil.

▶ Early strawberry flowers may need protecting from late frosts. A piece of horticultural fleece draped over the plants should do the trick.

### Repeat Sowing

No. Growing a combination of varieties that crop early and late will give the longest possible harvest, for example 'Florence' and 'Rosie' will give a long season of harvest.

### Ideal Conditions

Rich, deep soil in a sunny spot.

### Maintenance

Mulch plants with straw to keep the fruit clean and away from the soil. Growing plants through a black plastic mulch is a real time-saver. This has several advantages: it keeps the fruit clean, keeps the weeds down, and warms the soil. The disadvantages are that it is hard to water or mulch the plants and it looks unattractive. The problem of watering can be solved by fitting a soaker hose under the plastic sheet. White plastic sheet mulch is also available—this reflects light into the plants, helping the fruit to ripen and, it seems, deterring pests such as aphids. However, I prefer to stick with traditional straw.

Runners (small plants at the end of a long stem) are produced from the plants and should be removed (unless you need a new batch of plants) as they will take up valuable water and nutrients. If you do want a few extra plants and your existing strawberries are in good health, stake the rooted runners into pots of compost and keep them moist.

### When to Water

Water new plants until they are established, then water in prolonged dry spells and as the fruit is ripening. Water the soil, not the plant, as a deluge of water may damage the fruit.

### Common Problems and Solutions

**Birds** will start to eat your strawberry crop long before you want to harvest it, so protect the plants during fruiting with a mesh cloche. I will only use a chicken wire cloche, as birds can become tangled in other plastic fruit nettings—this is a length of chicken wire attached to wire arches, the same as I might use to protect brassicas from butterflies.

**Gray mold** can affect plants when conditions are too wet, but watering in the morning rather than evening can help.

Ready to enjoy, these 'Oregon Thornless' berries may not be the largest but they have a great taste.

# Blackberries ★ ★ ✮

Large, swollen, glossy cultivated blackberries could almost be a different fruit to those found in the hedgerow. They can take up a fair bit of growing space and do need training up some form of support, but they are really not fussy and will grow happily in partial shade. Beyond some very basic care and simple pruning, there is little to do except await the harvest. With berries ready in late summer and early autumn, the blackberry is a great way to extend the soft fruit period.

## Varieties to Try

**'Oregon Thornless'** is a compact variety suited to small spaces. As the name suggests, it lacks thorns, which is an advantage when it comes to pruning and harvesting, particularly if you have children helping. It produces a good crop of tasty berries from late summer to early autumn. The leaves are very pretty, being deeply cut and quite unlike the common bramble, making it a decorative way to cover fencing.

**'Waldo'** is an exceptionally compact thornless variety suited to smaller plots. Plants can be planted just 5 ft. (1.5 m) apart and the fruits they produce are truly exceptional. I grow 'Waldo' trained up a single vertical post.

**'Himalayan Giant'** is a monster of a plant, but if you have a fence to cover or need to generate a windbreak, then this spiny plant will do the job and give about 20 lb. (9 kg) of fruit, too.

## Spacing and Planting

If you aren't planning to train your blackberries up against a wall, fence, or shed, then you will need to build a post and wire support. Stretch 3–5 horizontal wires between two posts to make a support about 5 ft. (1.5 m) high. Plant them any time from late autumn through to the spring, and after planting cut the canes back to about 8 in. (20 cm).

## How Many?

The average plot is unlikely to have space for many blackberries, so thornless varieties that are more compact could be a good option and two plants might be reasonable. A compact thornless plant should deliver about 8 lb. (3.5 kg) of succulent berries once it is established. One 'Himalayan Giant' is probably more than enough for most families.

## Ideal Conditions

Blackberries like damp conditions and a soil with plenty of organic matter. They will grow in sun or shade, but fruit in the sun will be ready earlier and probably will be sweeter.

## Maintenance and Pruning

Mulch around the plant in early spring as part of the annual mulching of all beds. Don't pamper them, they don't need it. Blackberries are pruned in the same way as summer-fruiting raspberries; sometime after fruiting finishes and before spring, cut out all the canes that bore fruit and tie the new canes to the wires, training them horizontally along the wires. Choosing a thornless variety makes pruning less painful.

## When to Water

Until new plants are established.

## Common Problems and Solutions

The blackberry is a fairly trouble-free plant, though in theory it can be afflicted with many of the same problems as raspberries (see page 155). In damp weather, gray mold can develop on the fruit and the damaged fruit should be picked but not composted.

## Boysenberries, Tayberries, and Loganberries

These are all hybrids of the blackberry, raspberry, and dewberry. Their cultivation is similar to that of their parents.

◄ The shiny blackberry is brimming with antioxidants. It almost seems too good to be true, as it grows easily, is a real treat to eat, and is good for you.

# Black, Red, and White Currants ✦ ✦ ✧

Packed with vitamin C, black currants and their close relatives red and white currants are blissfully simple and trouble-free to grow. Jewel-like colors and powerful flavors make them a pleasure to cook with, although they are arguably less useful in the kitchen than other soft fruits and a little fiddly to prepare. The bushes will grow to 5 ft. (1.5 m) at most and can be used as an informal boundary.

◀ Black currants, crammed with vitamin C, are expensive to buy but incredibly fruitful once established. A weed-suppressing landscape fabric will eliminate the need for weeding.

## Varieties to Try
'Ben Connon' is an early black currant that delivers a heavy crop of the largest fruit.
'Ben Sarek' is a compact black currant that still gives a good harvest.
'White Grape' is a white currant with an excellent flavor.
'Red Lake' is a prolific, popular cultivar producing long trusses of gleaming red fruit.

## Plant or Seed?
Plants, bare-root or container-grown.

## Spacing and Planting
Plant with a gap of 5 ft. (1.5 m) between bushes. Plant bare-root black currant bushes with plenty of compost about 2 in. (5 cm) deeper than they were grown in the nursery.

## When to Plant
Late autumn to winter.

## When to Harvest
As fruits ripen.

## How Many?
A single bush will give plenty of currants.

## Repeat Sowing
If you have the space, growing different varieties will prolong the harvest.

## Ideal Conditions
Currants prefer an open situation with rich soil. Black currants are hungrier than red or white but will tolerate a little shade.

## Maintenance
Mulch around the bushes as part of the annual mulch. Protect the ripening fruit from birds. All currants are pruned in the winter. For black currants, remove about a third of the oldest stems (those with the darkest bark). Red and white currants should be pruned in the same way as gooseberries (see page 151).

## When to Water
Until new plants are established.

## Common Problems and Solutions
**Gall mites** living in the buds cause big bud, which is most noticeable in the spring as some buds grow fatter than others. These mites spread reversion disease and the affected stems should be removed and destroyed. Reversion disease causes buds to dry up and fall off rather than develop, stunting the leaves and reducing the yield. Unfortunately there is no cure and bushes have to be removed and destroyed.

A good red currant bush should yield 10 lb. (4.5 kg) of fruit—a great harvest for just 5 ft. (1.5 m) of space and a quick prune!

These 'Invicta' gooseberries, left on the plant to ripen, are just about sweet enough to eat without cooking.

# Gooseberries ✶ ✶ ⚹

One of the earliest fruits of the year, the gooseberry is an incredibly generous, unfussy plant and is a breeze to grow. It will occupy a permanent place in the vegetable garden, but the harvest it provides is worth the space, so long as you like the tart fruit. Gooseberries can be grown as ornamental half standards and still produce a hefty crop, and the space below can be used to grow a low-growing crop such as salad leaves or strawberries. Standards do well in very large pots but require more pampering.

A gooseberry bush can produce for as long as 20 years—a great return from just one plant.

### Varieties to Try

'**Invicta**' is a green, heavy-cropping variety that is resistant to mildew.
'**Hinnonmäki Yellow**' produces large, fragrant, yellow fruits that ripen in midsummer and is mildew resistant.
'**Hinnonmäki Red**' has glorious, flavorsome red fruits when allowed to ripen. This is a very hardy plant useful in very cold areas and is resistant to mildew.
'**Captivator**' is highly productive, thornless, and mildew resistant.

### Plant or Seed?

Plants, bare-root or container grown.

### Spacing and Planting

Plant with 3 ft. (1 m) between bushes and half standards.

### When to Plant

Autumn and winter.

### When to Harvest

Some fruit can be picked in late spring, green and startlingly sharp, for cooking. The remainder of the crop will then have more space to swell and ripen on the bush.

### How Many?

An established bush in a good year will produce 10 lb. (4.5 kg) of fruit, so one bush is probably enough.

### Repeat Sowing

No.

### Ideal Conditions

Fairly unfussy, will tolerate partial shade. Moisture-retentive soil.

### Maintenance

Mulch around bushes as part of the annual mulch. Standards need good strong support, especially as the fruits form, since the laden heads can literally bow down under the weight. Prune in the late autumn or winter. Bushes are grown on a leg (a short stem) and you are aiming for an open goblet shape by reducing the main branches by about a third of their length. Thornless cultivars are much easier to prune.

### When to Water

Until newly planted bushes are established.

### Common Problems and Solutions

**Gooseberry saw fly**, or rather its caterpillars, will strip a bush of foliage, starting from the center and working out. I left my standard gooseberries lush and green and returned a few days later to find them a forlorn bunch of twigs, but the bushes recovered and still produced some fruit. The caterpillars are dull green, about 1 in. (2.5 cm) long and easily visible. The best solution is vigilance; check the undersides of leaves from mid-spring onwards and pick off the caterpillars.
**American gooseberry mildew** produces a white powdery mildew on leaves and fruit. Affected shoots should be pruned out and destroyed. Opening up the structure of the bush to allow air to circulate can help. This is a very common problem and the best option is to grow one of the many excellent resistant varieties.

The obelisks supporting these raspberry plants are not only practical but can also serve as a boundary or divide in the garden.

# Raspberries ✦ ✦ ✦

Besides pruning and mulching once a year and possibly a little watering, there is really nothing to growing great raspberries. Even the pruning is straightforward. A short row will provide plenty of luscious, fragrant fruit for summery puddings. If I had only enough space to grow one soft fruit, I would choose raspberries for the ease with which they are grown and the delicious fruit. There are summer- and autumn-fruiting varieties; arguably those fruiting in the autumn are less work as they require no support and are susceptible to fewer problems, and even the pruning is simpler. Although referred to as autumn fruiting they will normally start providing fruit from mid summer, so when time and space are limited choosing to grow only autumn raspberries is sensible.

## Varieties to Try

'**Malling Jewel**' is a midsummer variety. It may not be the most prolific producer but I choose to grow it because it produces the most delicious fruit. The berries also last well on the canes—a good characteristic if you can only visit your plot once or twice a week.
'**Autumn Bliss**' is a prolific autumn-fruiting cultivar, producing a profusion of large tasty berries.

## Plant or Seed?

Plants, as bare-root canes.

## Spacing and Planting

If you order your plants by mail order, they will probably arrive looking like a fairly shabby bundle of dry sticks with roots at one end. Raspberries need good, rich soil in a sheltered, sunny spot, although they will put up with some shade. Dig a shallow trench 2–3 ⅛ in. (5–8 cm) deep, place the canes in the trench about 12 in. (30 cm) apart, spread out their roots, and backfill the trench with soil, firming the soil around the canes. If the canes are longer than about 12 in. (30 cm), cut them back to this height to a bud.

Summer-fruiting varieties will grow very tall and need some form of support. I grow mine up the deer fence, which works well and hides it for a while, but they can be grown up obelisks or, perhaps most practically, against two or three horizontal lengths of wire stretched between two posts. Supports need to be about 6 ft. (1.8 m) high. A nice row of raspberries can be used as a boundary or divide in the garden.

## When to Plant

Autumn or early winter.

## When to Harvest

There are summer- and autumn-fruiting varieties available.

## How Many?

Twelve plants, a row of about 16 ft. (5 m), should give a good crop, although half this number could be worthwhile. Raspberries will be a permanent part of the garden and they could be delivering a good crop of raspberries for up to ten years, so it is important to get the location and quantity right. It is also worth

Pick ripe raspberries as often as you can to encourage new fruits to form.

considering how much shade summer-fruiting raspberries might create on neighboring beds before planning a permanent bed.

## Repeat Sowing
No.

## Ideal Conditions
Raspberries thrive in good, fertile soil with plenty of organic matter. They struggle in chalky soil. A sunny, sheltered spot in the garden will give the best harvest.

## Maintenance
Mulch around the canes (the name for raspberry stems) with good garden compost in the annual mulch. When the canes reach the top of their supports, snip off the tip of the cane a few centimeters above the support.

Summer-fruiting varieties should be pruned once all the fruit has been picked. Fruit is produced on canes that grew last season, so all the canes that bore fruit can be cut away to just above ground level, leaving the new canes to produce fruit the following year. The new canes can be thinned out by taking out the weakest and leaving the canes about 4 in. (10 cm) apart. I have seen pictures in books where this all seems to work out perfectly, with equally sized canes, equally spaced. Mine never quite work like that, but the harvest is still good.

Autumn-fruiting varieties are easier to prune as all the canes are cut to just above ground level in very late winter. Again, traditionally the new canes would be thinned, but it doesn't seem to be a problem if all the canes are left to fruit.

## When to Water
Water well if it is dry when the canes are in flower and the fruits are swelling.

## Common Problems and Solutions
**Birds** are perhaps the most difficult problem once the fruit begins to ripen, and they will take them long before we would consider them to be ripe. As soon as your crop is anywhere near ripe, use every method you can to keep the birds from feasting before you do. Several options are suggested on page 187.

**Raspberry beetle** is another common pest on summer-fruiting cultivars. The beetle lays its eggs in the flower and the larvae eat into the stalk end of the fruit, causing a dried brown or distorted area on the berry near the stalk. Without spraying, which is only effective when carried out at absolutely the right moment, there is little that can be done in the short term. Disturbing the surface of the soil around the plants throughout the winter should go some way to disturbing the life cycle of the beetle and cutting down numbers for the following year. If the problem recurs, try autumn-fruiting varieties that flower at a time when the beetles are not laying eggs.

**Viruses and fungal infections** can unfortunately reduce the vigor of the plants and the size of the harvest. Once the problem becomes too great and the harvest too small, the best solution is to start again in a new location with new canes.

**Chlorosis**, a yellowing of the leaves, will occur if the soil is too limey.

◀ Raspberries are such a favorite in my family that I added a few canes up some simple homemade obelisks of painted 3 x 3 ft. (1 x 1 m) lumber and tied with synthetic rope to supplement the main bed. The wind chime is an attempt to deter deer!

# Edible Flowers

**Borage • Chives • Calendula • Zucchini (Courgette) Flowers • Lavender
Nasturtiums • Viola Odorata**

There are several reasons for growing flowers in the vegetable garden: to cut and enjoy in the house, to encourage beneficial insects, and because they can bring a different dimension to your dinner table. Edible flowers are unlikely to be your main focus in the vegetable plot, but having a few tasty blooms to garnish food and drinks really makes them special. Edible blooms are like anything else, only grow the ones you enjoy and will use. I also add the condition that they have to be useful for something else, too, either for cutting or as a companion plant. Space in the vegetable garden is precious, so I want the maximum from everything. Below is a short list of edible flowers you may like to try—the list is in no way exhaustive but includes the blooms I have found most useful and easy to grow.

## Borage

Essential for summer drinks. An annual that can be planted as a small plant in late spring, although once you have it, it will probably self-seed readily. Use the flowers fresh or encase them in gleaming ice cubes.

## Chives

A culinary herb with the bonus of having very pretty purple flowers that will add a touch of oniony zing to salads and omelets. The leaves appear in late winter and the flowers in late spring. They are perennial, easy to grow, and are also useful companion plants as they repel aphids.

## Calendula

The thin orange or yellow petals of the calendula are lovely scattered on a green salad. Calendula is also a fantastic companion plant and grows easily from seed planted in mid-spring. Self-seeds readily.

**Clockwise from left** Chives, borage, and calendula.

## Lavender

Lavender can be a permanent part of the vegetable garden. I have used the plants to provide a decorative end to my long beds, three to a bed. Lavender brings hordes of bees to the garden and can be used to flavor shortbread, sugar, ice creams, and preserves. Lavender needs a sunny spot with well-drained soil.

## Zucchini (Courgette) Flowers

If you are growing zucchinis (courgettes) for the fruits, it won't do any harm to enjoy a few flowers. In fact, if you are experiencing a glut, taking a few flowers will keep the harvest going without producing more fruits. The star-shaped flowers can be stuffed, baked, or dipped in batter and deep-fried. (See pages 113–114 for cultivation.)

▲ Lavender

▶ Zucchini (courgette) flower

## Nasturtiums

There are numerous varieties of nasturtiums in shades of yellow, orange, and velvety mahogany. They, too, are a useful companion plant. The flowers, leaves, and even the green seed pods are edible, having a strong, peppery taste. They can be grown easily from direct sown seed in mid-spring and will probably self-seed.

## Viola Odorata

These pretty, delicate flowers will smarten up any average salad or soup, while the crystallized flower will make even a simple cupcake special. They earn their place in the garden because they are the only edible flower to be had in late winter and early spring. I grow mine in large pots so they don't get swamped.

**Clockwise from left** Nasturtium, viola, fairy cake decorated with viola.

# PART IV

# How to Grow

I often remind myself that seeds are designed to germinate and grow into plants, and that these plants, given half a chance, will produce the fruits, bulbs, and roots that we love to eat. So if you have chosen to grow robust survivors in your low-maintenance vegetable garden, even if you only manage the bare minimum of care, you should get a crop that makes the time you have spent worthwhile. The key is in wading through the wealth of horticultural information and received wisdom and getting to the bare essentials of what is really necessary, figuring out what works for you on your plot, employing a few nifty shortcuts, and gaining the confidence to experiment. This chapter deals with the basics of how to grow vegetables and how to manage your plot in the most time-efficient manner, and as such there is nothing on grafting, propagation, or cross-pollinating but instead an explanation of the fundamentals of gardening, such as when to water, feed, and weed and how to get a fine tilth the quick way.

# Soil

The most important element in making your vegetable garden easy to manage and productive is getting the soil right. My grandfather always said, "Spend a little on the plant and a lot on the soil," pithily summing up gardening priorities and the fact that no matter how much you invest in seeds and plants, if your soil is not in "good heart" it will be wasted. Good, healthy soil is rich in nutrients and contains plenty of organic matter. It has an open structure, is able to hold onto moisture, and yet lets any excess drain away. It will be home to a whole host of creatures beneficial to the soil—bacteria, mites, worms, fungi, and centipedes are just a few—all of which help in the process of breaking down organic matter into humus. Worms are brilliant for the soil, aerating it as they drag down organic matter and help to break it down. Ideally, 18 in. (45 cm) of great soil is perfect for the vegetable garden. A healthy soil is easy to cultivate and produces robust plants that will survive a little damage from pests and put up a good fight against disease. Walking on the soil, especially when it is wet, can compact it and ruin its structure.

## Getting Great Soil

You are pretty much stuck with the mineral content of your soil—it is down to the geology of your area—but the depth, structure, and fertility can be improved by the addition of plenty of organic matter, such as well-rotted manure, garden compost, and leaf mold. Whether you are working on heavy or light soils, organic matter is the key because it opens up the structure of heavy soils, prevents it from clogging together, improves drainage and the fertility of light soils, adds bulk, and makes the soil more moisture retentive. Protecting light soils with a layer of mulch can also stop nutrients from being washed away. Heavy clay soils can be improved with the addition of plenty of grit to improve drainage. There are no quick fixes; your first efforts will make a difference, but each year that the soil is cultivated and improved it will become better and healthier, and this is an ongoing task. No-dig gardening protects the soil's structure and promotes fertility, and over a number of years will really improve any soil.

Heavy soils such as clay soils are heavy to work, sticky in wet weather, bake into hard clods in the sun,

and form a solid lump when scrunched in your hand. The good news is they are normally rich in nutrients, although it is slow to warm in the spring.

Light soils such as silty or sandy soils feel gritty but are free-draining and light and easy to work. These soils tend to dry out quickly and are poor in nutrients, which are leached away.

If you want a quick route to better soil or if your soil is very difficult, the simplest solution is to construct a set of raised beds about 12–18 in. (30–45 cm) deep, buy in some excellent topsoil, and fill your beds with a mix of garden compost, topsoil, and well-rotted manure, and instantly you have a good depth of rich topsoil perfect for growing vegetables. Check the quality of the topsoil you are buying as it would be a shame to buy in the same problems you have already. If your garden is very poorly drained the beds can be even deeper, 24 in. (60 cm) or more, and the ground below the beds needs to be dug over and a fair amount of gravel incorporated to ensure the beds can drain properly and don't become bog gardens.

## THE BASICS

Invest in creating good soil. Good soil gives great returns and makes every aspect of growing your own easier.

Humble, homemade garden compost helps many problem soils; heavy, badly drained, light, and infertile soils all benefit from a good dose of compost.

# No-Dig Gardening

No-dig gardening is the easiest, least time-consuming way to manage the soil, perfect for the vegetable grower with little time to spare, and the good news is that this is not a shortcut that compromises the fertility or quality of your soil. It is actually fantastic for the soil structure and feeding the living soil.

Digging the vegetable garden in the autumn and leaving the clods to be broken down by frost over the winter is the traditional way to manage the soil. In reality there are plenty of reasons not to dig; it destroys the soil structure, causes compaction (hence the clods that need breaking up), lowers fertility by speeding up the rate at which organic matter breaks down, exposes weed seeds, and it is time-consuming, backbreaking hard work. The no-dig method is just as it suggests—instead of hours of turning soil, the soil is covered with a layer of good garden compost or well-rotted farmyard manure, and the worms do the work by moving the mulch down into the soil where its nutrients can be released. I call it the annual mulch. Simple, natural, and relatively effortless for the gardener.

If you are growing in raised beds this system works perfectly, as you should be starting with a free-draining mixture of topsoil and organic matter. If you are working in low beds with poor drainage, this has to be addressed before you begin (see page 164). The nutrient-rich mulch should be applied to all beds in a layer at least 2 in. (5 cm) thick each year in late winter or very early spring before other tasks in the garden begin. For me this is like creating a beautiful blank canvas ready for planting. All I have to do is nip out and put the plants in as they arrive because all the preparation is done. Mulching and getting the garden ready like this does take a fair amount of time. It is a bit of a ritual: I normally set aside two half days early in the year for a good tidy-up of debris from the previous year and to tackle any weeds and mulch the beds. At the end of the process everything is shipshape, looking tidy and ready for the new growing season. Applying mulch before this, in the autumn, means that by the time you have plants growing in the beds a lot of the nutrients will have leached away over the winter. There is a case for mulching in the growing season, but I have found it is easier and effective to schedule in this intensive period of preparation, so that if all that follows is done in haste and piecemeal, I know the basics are done well. I mulch around all permanent fixtures such as raspberries and artichokes at the same time. There are just a couple of rules to follow—do not put mulch on if the ground is frozen or if the ground is water-logged and avoid mulching the beds where you intend to grow carrots and onions (if you did not opt for an autumn planting).

## THE BASICS

**No autumn digging. The whole growing area is covered with a 2 in. (5 cm) layer of garden compost or well-rotted manure in late winter or early spring.**

◄ A good layer of organic matter spread on vegetable beds early in the year is the cornerstone of remarkably simple and successful organic no-dig gardening.

► My plot has flourished under a time-saving, no-dig regime—a shortcut that is actually better for the soil.

# Marvelous Mulch

The act of applying a layer of mulch to the soil around plants is one of the most brilliant yet simple strategies for saving time in the vegetable patch. Beyond the universal annual mulching of the garden with nutrient-rich compost and farmyard manure, using all kinds of mulches in different situations is immensely useful throughout the growing season. If at any time an area is empty, a covering of sheet mulch will keep it pristine and weed free until you are ready to use it.

Mulch is a term used to describe anything that is used to cover the soil; this might be rich in nutrients, or just a sheet of black plastic to suppress weeds. The term "floating mulch" is even used to describe a layer of horticultural fleece draped over salad leaves to protect them from aphids or flea beetle. Mulches have three main functions—some achieve all three while others are more restricted: mulches feed the soil, suppress weeds,

and help retain moisture, all good news for the time-poor gardener. Applying them is quick and simple and can be as easy as tipping your grass cuttings onto a vegetable bed instead of the compost heap. There are plenty of materials, most without cost, that make excellent mulches, and they are my single greatest ally in my fight against weeds. It is a fact worth remembering that mulching is quicker and easier than weeding, and plants generally thrive in the conditions suitable mulch creates.

## Types of Mulch

### Garden Compost

Used in late winter or early spring as part of the no-dig system (see page 166), I apply a good covering around plants such as zucchinis (courgettes), pumpkins, and celeriac when I plant them. The true nutritional value of your compost will probably vary from barrow load to barrow load, but in general it supplies plants with both long-term and short-term nutrition, improves the soil's structure and its ability to hold onto moisture, and improves soil biodiversity. The more woody waste that goes into the compost, the less nutritious it will be. It may look a little rough and lumpy as it goes onto the soil, but it doesn't take long for the worms to set to work pulling it down into the soil.

### Well-Rotted Farmyard Manure

All farmyard manure must be well rotted before it is applied to the soil. This means it will be at least six months old, possibly a year. Many farmers and stables are only too pleased to give away manure, but be prepared to fill the sacks yourself. Like garden compost this should only be used in the general mulching of beds for fertility, not where the aim is to only suppress weeds.

### Leaf Mold

Leaf mold is a great soil conditioner; it does not add nutrients to the soil but adds organic bulk, opening its structure and increasing its ability to hold water. A blanket of leaf mold between rows of vegetables at least 7 in. (5 cm) thick is excellent for suppressing weeds and preventing the evaporation of valuable moisture from the soil. As with garden compost it is one of the incredibly useful ways of recycling free garden waste into something valuable. In fact, making leaf mold is even simpler than making compost.

▲ Straw is an inexpensive option if you have to buy mulch. Placed around these sweet corn it will suppress weeds, keep in moisture, and eventually break down into the soil.

## Grass Cuttings

Spreading cut grass straight onto the vegetable garden is just as easy as tipping it into the compost heap. Another garden waste product that can be put back into the garden, the cuttings will benefit the soil and save the gardener time. As with leaf mold, a layer 2–3 in. (5–7.5 cm) thick will prevent some evaporation from the soil and help to stop weeds from growing, while also adding valuable nutrients to the soil. Don't be tempted to pile on the grass cuttings too thickly, as the grass at the bottom may be deprived of oxygen and rot anaerobically, forming an unpleasant slime. I have used grass cuttings to cut down the weeding around beans, brassicas, rhubarb, cucurbits, and artichokes. They quickly fade to brown and eventually disappear into the soil. In summer grass cuttings are likely to be in good supply, but only use them once or twice on the same bed as they may add too much nitrogen to the soil.

## Newspaper, Cardboard, and Purpose-Made Paper Mulch

Newspaper and cardboard are laid on the soil to prevent weed growth. The newspaper needs to be several sheets thick, anchored in place with stones or by burying the edges in the soil, and watered thoroughly as soon as it is put down. This really doesn't look great and takes a while to put down but it really works, lasting a season, and can then be left to rot into the soil. To smarten it up a thin layer of hay, straw, or compost could be added, but that is more work, mulching twice over. Deliberately made rolls of paper for organic gardeners are available that look a good deal tidier but are fairly costly.

## Straw

If you are short of compost, have no leaf mold, and are faced with the prospect of having to buy some mulch material, then straw is a good option. It is inexpensive, very quick to get onto beds, is heavy enough to stay in place for the most part, and reflects light onto ripening fruit. A reasonable layer will keep weeds at bay, warm the soil, and help to preserve moisture.

## Black Plastic

Available cut from a large roll at most garden centers, hardware stores, or DIY shops, heavyweight black plastic is a versatile, reusable mulch, effective in preventing weed growth. It can be spread over the soil, anchored securely by burying the edges in the soil or held down with stones. Young plants can be planted into the soil beneath by cutting holes in the plastic. In very warm areas this can have the unwanted side effect of baking the soil, but it can be used to an advantage in colder areas at the end of the winter to warm the soil for early planting. The plastic is expensive but it can be reused and it certainly does work, although it doesn't look particularly appealing. I have mainly used this method to warm the soil, to grow potatoes, and around strawberry plants, where I hide the plastic with a more traditional mulch of straw.

## Mushroom Compost

This is a by-product of the mushroom-growing industry that is available to buy in bulk. A generous layer will suppress weeds, keep the moisture in, and add organic bulk to the soil, but its nutrient content is minimal. It is beautifully dark and crumbly and leaves beds looking fantastic, but the expense of buying it makes it less preferable than other mulches.

## Seaweed

Gathered from the seashore, seaweed is full of all kinds of nutrients that will be valuable in promoting fine growth in the vegetable plot. Few people are likely to have a vast supply, and so adding a thick layer to thwart weeds is probably not an option. Seaweed dries out quickly and shrinks, leaving gaps, but a thin layer works well to give soil an extra boost. It should be washed thoroughly first to remove some of the salt.

## Wood Ash

So long as no plastics have gone onto the firewood, ash is a useful mulch high in potash, and is good for fruiting plants.

## THE BASICS

A mulch is anything that is used to cover the soil. Generally mulches prevent weed growth, help retain moisture, and sometimes improve the soil.

# Feeding and Fertilizers

In a well-run, organic, no-dig garden with a good regime of applying mulch, very little extra feeding is necessary as your soil should contain all a plant needs to thrive. With the constant introduction of organic matter into the soil, you are feeding the soil using natural products and natural processes, which then feeds the plant. The nutrients removed with every plant you grow, or leached away through the soil, are replaced by the rotting organic matter. However, there are some circumstances, especially in new gardens, in which some feeding may be required to get a good, healthy crop or where well-judged feeding can significantly increase yield. The vegetable plot is the area of the garden where the most is asked of the soil and keeping it fertile is vital. Blanket, routine feeding, however, can be a waste of valuable time and money; in fact, it can be detrimental, encouraging the wrong type of growth, too much leaf instead of fruit, or soft growth that is more prone to disease.

As a belt-and-braces measure in new gardens, you could use a little broad-spectrum organic fertilizer developed for the vegetable garden when you plant or sow seed. A general fertilizer will probably contain roughly similar quantities of nitrogen, phosphates, and potassium. In bald terms, nitrogen promotes leafy growth, phosphates are good for roots, and potassium promotes flowering and fruit. There is a whole range of fertilizers developed for the vegetable patch and each has a different make up of nutrients tailored to the requirements of different plants—you could quite easily buy a specific fertilizer for every crop. It is reassuring to imagine that you have exactly the right product for each crop, but for the most part it is unnecessary because soil in good condition will do the work for you.

Confident that my soil is up to the job, my extra feeding regime is limited to tomatoes and cucumbers, and then I confess it is a little erratic, consisting of the occasional liquid seaweed feed.

## THE BASICS

In an established, organic, no-dig garden, very little extra feeding is required.

▶ It makes sense to plant leafy brassicas in soil enriched by a crop of legumes. The brassicas can exploit the nitrogen left behind by the previous crop.

## What and When to Feed

If production or growth is slow for any plant, use a liquid seaweed feed or perhaps foliar spray—this is one of the best ways to get nutrients and trace elements to plants. The results should be fast and noticeable. Plants that respond well to regular feeding are listed below:

- **Zucchinis (courgettes):** Dilute high potash tomato food. Only if production is slow.
- **Brassicas:** Nitrogen fixed by peas. Not feeding by the gardener but worth noting that brassicas do benefit from this fix of nitrogen.

- **Peppers:** High potash tomato food. Once a week when the fruits form.
- **Eggplants (aubergines):** High potash tomato food. Once a week when the fruits form.
- **Tomatoes:** High potash tomato food. Once a week.

- **Cucumbers:** Balanced feed. Once a week once harvesting begins.
- **Beans** (all types) High potash feed. A couple of times once harvesting begins to prolong harvesting.

In the low-maintenance vegetable garden the only seeds to use are those that can be sown directly into the soil where they are to germinate and grow without much fuss. Most small seeds like carrots, radishes, and salad leaves are sown in shallow furrows created by dragging a hoe, a trowel, or your hand through the soil. For the beginner, one of the best pieces of advice I can give is keep your row straight. Initially I let my creative side and the urge not to follow the rules get the better of me and tried planting in clever shapes and rows that meandered, but this was a mistake. Weeding with a hoe was impossible and in the early stages deciding which were the seedlings I wanted and which were weeds was tricky. Seedlings in orderly, poker-straight rows are easy to hoe and the invading weeds are easily spotted. It looks neat, too. I still plant for an attractive mix of leaves and colors where I can, but in straight rows. To keep plants in line use a cane, a garden line, or a homemade board marked with centimeter or inch measurements to help with spacing.

For seeds requiring a furrow, first mark out your furrows to about the right depth and gently water the furrow with a watering can with a fine rose if the soil is dry. Next, sprinkle the seeds thinly along the furrow—

don't shake them from the packet as the likelihood is hundreds of seeds will land in the same spot. Instead, pour a few seeds into one hand and sprinkle into the furrow with the other, a pinch at a time. Finally, gently shuffle the soil back over the furrow. Put in a label right away. If you only sow a part row, leaving space for a repeat sowing, stick a marker where the first planting finishes.

## A Shortcut to a Fine Tilth

Packets of small seeds will undoubtedly suggest that the soil is worked to a fine tilth before sowing, meaning a soil that is fine and free from large lumps. This makes sense as small seeds can be washed through a lumpy soil and therefore need to be surrounded by warm, damp soil to germinate successfully. They will be far more successful in putting down roots and throwing up shoots if they don't encounter large, hard clods or dry cavities. However, achieving a fine tilth is not always easy. Even if you pull aside the most recent layer of mulch the soil may still look inhospitable, especially if it is still new to cultivation. So here is a quick solution—draw out a furrow three or four times the depth required, fill it with an organic seed compost or mole hills if you have them, sow the seeds as above, and fill the furrow with the same compost. (Moles are a nuisance but mole hills contain the most beautifully fine soil, perfect for seeds.) Effectively, what you have done is planted your seeds in a container of perfect compost, one that their roots can grow straight out of into fertile soil when they are ready.

Larger seeds such as beans and zucchinis (courgettes) can be planted by simply pushing them gently into the ground to the right depth. Packets normally recommend planting two seeds at each spot to allow for any seeds that fail to germinate. The weakest seedling at each station can then be removed, leaving the more robust plant to grow. Pull out the weakling gently so as not to damage the remaining plant.

◀ These tiny carrot seeds are hard to handle. Pour a few seeds into one hand and sprinkle pinches with the other to avoid wasting seed.

▲ Tiny kale seeds need good contact with the soil to germinate well, so I use the shortcut to a fine tilth by creating a channel of potting compost and pulling back the rough mulch so I am sowing them in the perfect growing medium.

▲ Pencil bean seeds can be sown by pushing them into the soil. Sow a couple at each spot in case one seed fails to germinate.

◄ Large robust seeds such as these runner beans can simply be pushed into the soil.

# Collecting Seed

Collecting and storing your own seed is a thrifty trick. It is simplest with peas and beans because a few pods can be left on the plants to dry at the end of the season and gathered before the damper weather comes. The seed can be stored in brown envelopes or paper bags with the cultivar names written on, in a cool, dark place. Other plants are less straightforward; crops such as carrots, for example, require you to allow some carrots to flower and set seed. I have never found this worthwhile. Saving a few potatoes for the following year's crop is possible but you run the risk of a buildup of viruses or disease, so I always opt for those from a reputable supplier. Saving a few Jerusalem artichokes makes sense, and to save time they can be treated like perennials by just throwing a few tubers back when you harvest. It is also worth remembering that the seed of an F1 hybrid will not come true; that is, the plants will not share the characteristics of the parents.

Beans are the easiest seed to collect. They are large, easy to handle, and come packed in neat pods. I grow beans for their seed pods, but some other plants such as carrots and onions have to be allowed to run to seed before any can be collected.

# Planting

This is pretty straightforward. Ensure the plant is recently watered, dig out a small hole to fit the plant root ball, pop in the plant, check that the soil level is the same as in the original container, and gently push the soil around the root ball. Use a watering can with a fine rose to water it in. There are a few exceptions: young leeks are dropped into a hole made with a dibble (see pages 138–139), sweet corn need planting slightly deeper than in their original pots to encourage rooting, zucchinis (courgettes) and pumpkins can be planted up to the level of their seed leaves (the first pair of leaves the plant grows), and brassicas need to be planted deeply and really firmed in well, perhaps with your heel, to thrive. Use a line or board as with sowing seed to keep rows straight and easy to weed. Keep the young plants watered if the weather is dry and protect them with cloches or fleece if the weather is cold until they are established. If you can, choose to plant out on a dull day so the plants lose less moisture.

Young plants take only a few moments to get into the ground, but take care not to damage their root systems.

# Spacing

very seed packet and plant label will have recommendations for spacing between plants and between rows of plants. Most gardening books also suggest spacing, too, and it wouldn't be uncommon for there to be disagreements. Spacing crops is important to ensure that each plant gets enough light, nutrients, and water to grow well and to allow easy weeding between plants and rows. It follows that in fertile, well-drained, moisture-retentive soil (such as in well-maintained raised beds) plants can thrive with less space than in poorer, dry soils and give the best possible harvest from the area you cultivate. Using growing space effectively is like packing the plants in the most efficient way, and staggering plants in neighboring rows usually gives a tight, economical fit.

The distance at which one plant grows from another can influence its size. This can be useful as you may want to grow a large number of smaller onions rather than fewer larger ones, or cabbages or carrots, or perhaps some of each. I deliberately plant my cabbages very close together, producing two or three per person, as two of my children have yet to be persuaded that cabbage is edible. Closer spacing can also help to keep the beds covered, leaving less space for weeds. Leafy plants such as zucchinis (courgettes) will cover the ground, preventing weeds from growing. So spacing is not as rigid as you may imagine. The range of spacing for each crop is suggested on pages 48–161, but don't be afraid to use common sense and experiment within reason, or adapt spacing to the practicalities of your beds.

## Catch Crops

Beyond packing plants effectively, it makes sense to generate as much harvest as you can from the space available. Growing a fast-maturing crop among a slower-growing crop gives two or perhaps three harvests out of one area without compromising on the quality of either. The fast-growing crop is known as a catch crop, and radishes, beets (beetroot), salad leaves, spring onions, and lettuces all make good catch crops. Filling the space also allows less room for weeds to grow.

▶ These young cabbages will take a while to mature. In the meantime fast-growing crops such as radishes, spring onions, or beets (beetroot) can be grown between the plants to make the most of the space.

# Weeding

Probably the least loved task in the vegetable plot, it is also incredibly satisfying. A freshly weeded bed with a smart row of vibrant plants looks fantastic. Weeds are thieves of the moisture, nutrition, and light that should be going into producing your vegetables, and they need to be removed as soon as possible. Weeds also provide a haven for pests and can carry diseases that can affect your crops, such as clubroot that affects brassicas. However, I have accepted that a weed-free plot is something that for now I can only dream of, and instead I have developed a pragmatic approach to dealing with weeds. Prevention is easier than cure, so I mulch wherever I can to deprive weed seeds of the light they need to germinate and also whizz around with the hoe. I concentrate on keeping the crops that are more likely to be affected by an infestation of weeds—such as onions, shallots, and carrots—weed free by shallow hoeing once a week or once a fortnight in the growing season, which only takes about five or ten minutes each time. Some crops such as zucchinis (courgettes), rhubarb, and pumpkins are likely to shade the weeds out, their vast leaves depriving weeds of light rather than vice versa, and will continue to produce with a few weeds around. Well-established and nourished fruit canes or bushes will also tolerate a few weeds and continue to give a good crop. So in these situations weeds are less of a problem and can be ignored for a while, but they have to be tackled eventually.

As well as spending my weeding time on the crops most likely to be damaged by the competition, I also look out for the worst weeds. It is worth getting to know weeds and their habits. Annual weeds are not so much of a hazard; they are usually easy to pull out and can be thwarted by chopping the tops off with a hoe. The real difficulty comes when annuals flower and set seed as they can produce hundreds of seeds all programmed to germinate where they fall in your vegetable plot, so annual weeds need to be removed before they set seed, and the same goes for perennials such as dandelions. I once walked across a swath of grass with a seasoned head gardener, and as we walked he regularly bobbed down to pick off the heads of dandelions. The plant might have remained but he had prevented thousands of seeds from being distributed through the garden. So if all else fails simply pick off the flower heads, which only takes a few seconds, buying you a little time. Perennial weeds that spread underground and pop up all over the garden, such as ground elder and creeping buttercup, present a different challenge. Left to spread they can get really established, ensnaring your plants in a mesh of roots that takes time and patience to remove. So it is common sense to tackle these as soon as you can and make an effort to wheedle out all the roots that you can get to, as even a small section left in the ground can regrow.

Bindweed has a root system that may extend several meters (yards) into the soil, so the only option is to remove as much of it as you can when it pops up and keep on top of it in the hope that it will finally run out of steam. Few people can keep a weed-free plot; just spend what time you have to remove the weeds that matter, and mulch and hoe as much as you can to prevent the weed problem before it germinates.

## Know Your Weeds

- **Annuals:** chickweed, groundsel, hairy bittercress, annual nettle, and fat hen.
- **Perennials:** docks, dandelions, and brambles.
- **Particularly invasive perennials needing immediate action:** creeping buttercup, ground elder, couch grass, bindweed, and horsetail.

### Hoeing

This may seem like a task that really doesn't need discussion. However, there are a couple of points worth knowing. If you have time, hoe between carrots and onions even if the soil appears to be free of weeds, as this will remove the growing tips of weeds before they break the surface. If you are hoeing off young seedlings, ensure they cannot re-root—if you can, hoe on a warm, sunny day when roots will shrivel in the sun. Finally, hoe as shallowly as possible so as not to bring up more weed seeds into the light where they can germinate.

◀ A good sharp hoe will slice through weeds cleanly, removing the growing tips. Regular hoeing is quick and easy and far less work than weeding once the weeds are established.

# Watering

The exact amount of time and effort you need to spend watering or setting your irrigation system to water will depend on your local climactic conditions, particularly how moisture-retentive you have managed to make your soil and the vagaries of the weather in any particular year. In general, however, once plants are established they require watering less often than might be expected, and a great deal of time can be saved by knowing what to water and when watering will significantly increase the harvest a crop produces. Watering frugally encourages plants to develop a good root system, sending roots deep into the soil in search of water, and this in turn makes them more able to gather moisture and nutrients from the soil, rendering them less reliant on being watered and more drought tolerant. A seasoned vegetable grower I know described watering the vegetable garden as "making a rod for your own back," and in the low-maintenance plot less work is the aim, so watering cannily pays off. Overwatering can affect the taste of some crops, literally diluting the taste, and possibly make them more susceptible to diseases and encourage slugs and snails. Too much water can also compact the soil and wash away the nutrients you have worked hard to get into the soil. Often a good soaking just once a week is enough for most crops, if at all.

I water very little, as I garden a moisture-retentive soil in an area with a generally favorable climate and reasonable rainfall. It is hard to be dogmatic as many factors will affect the need to water, but here are some guidelines:

- Recently transplanted young plants and newly emerged seedlings will need to be watered, especially in very warm weather, until they are established.

- A good deluge once a week or every ten days, depending on the weather conditions, should be sufficient for most vegetables. This is preferable to watering more frequently in small amounts as this encourages surface rooting, which in turn makes plants more reliant on watering. Most plants draw water from the top 12 in. (30 cm) of soil, so aim to keep that moist. The surface may look dry but that is irrelevant to your vegetables—the condition of the soil several inches down is what matters.

- Focus on watering when it really counts. Some plants such as leafy brassicas, spinach, and salad leaves need a steady supply of water, while others in the list on page 181 will produce a much heavier crop if they are watered at the key time, usually when flowering and fruit are being produced. Also water any wilting plants, as this is a sign that moisture levels are low.

- It is better to water very early in the morning rather than at night or in the heat of the day. Water applied in the heat of the day will be likely to evaporate before it does any good or scorch the leaves, and watering at night engenders the kind of damp environment that encourages slugs and snails and can cause molds.

- Water the soil, not the plant, as delicate leaves can be damaged or rot if blasted with a watering can or sprinkler. Use a fine rose on a watering can or drip or spray delivery nozzles on an irrigation system to avoid washing away the soil and prevent the water from running off rather than seeping into the soil.

- If it rains enough there is no need to water, but light showers in warm or windy weather may not actually be enough to really wet the soil.

- Watering with rainwater is best for the plants and the environment, and your pocket if you are on a water meter. A few simple rain barrels under downspouts from the house, garage, and shed roofs will collect sufficient rainwater for watering, although increasingly complex rainwater harvesting systems are available with below-ground tanks to service the needs of the garden and some parts of the house. Submersible pumps are available for rain barrels that can be connected to an irrigation system. Gray water collected from the house should not be used in the vegetable patch as it is likely to contain residues of cleaning products.

▲ This much-loved watering can has a very fine rose ideal for gently watering around young plants and seedlings.

## Plants Needing Plenty of Water:
- Zucchinis (courgettes)
- Squashes
- Pumpkins
- Runner beans
- Salad leaves and lettuces
- Cucumbers

## Plants to Water at Key Times When Fruits Are Swelling:
- Fava beans (broad beans)
- Peas
- Green beans (French beans)
- Raspberries
- Strawberries
- Tomatoes

## Plants That Seldom Need Watering:
- Carrots
- Beets (beetroot) and most root crops
- Onions
- Shallots
- Garlic
- Rhubarb
- Jerusalem artichokes
- Artichokes

# Crop Rotation

Not growing the same crop in the same bed each year is common sense. Each crop removes a slightly different set of nutrients from the soil, and repeatedly growing the same crop in the same area would deplete the special mix of nutrients that crop requires. Pests and diseases associated with the crop will build up in the soil and become an intractable problem. So it is logical to leave it as long as possible before growing a crop or closely related crops in the same bed. Some gardeners find that three years works well, others four. If you have a real problem with a particular disease, leave it as long as you can before returning the same crop to that bed. That is basically all you really need to know.

This is one of the areas where keeping a good notebook or set of plans helps, recording what grew where over several seasons, especially if you use catch crops and attractive patterns that can be difficult to remember. I get my plans out when I put in my orders for plants and seeds and make up one for that year, ensuring I have enough space for everything and in a different spot from where it grew previously.

There are a whole host of rules that you can follow, with crops divided into groups and the order in which they should follow each other set out. All very sensible and with very sound horticultural reasons behind them, but the likelihood is that in reality it will be hard to adhere to for a number of reasons. Firstly, the exact growing space required by one group may not be identical to that required by the group that follows, and you may want to grow more cabbages than peas, or maybe no cabbages at all. Secondly, crops such as runner beans and Jerusalem artichokes can only occupy certain spots in the garden if they are not to cast a shadow over other beds. And thirdly, you may just not have enough space for the system to work. The small plot has little space between beds and so diseases and pests might easily travel. Some diseases such as clubroot persist in the soil for tens of years so can't be outmaneuvered!

Having said all that, here are the pared-down rules to aspire to. Grouped for a three-year rotation, crops follow each other in numerical order. A four-year rotation subdivides the groups further.

## Group 1
**Roots** such as carrots, leeks, onions, beets (beetroot), and shallots.

## Group 2
**Podded and fruiting vegetables** such as peas, beans, zucchinis (courgettes), cucumbers, pumpkins, and sweet corn.

## Group 3
**Brassicas** such as broccoli, cabbages, kale, and radishes.

## Other Crops Can Be Slotted In Anywhere
A major advantage of rotation is that the character of one crop can be used to benefit the next. Podded vegetables fix nitrogen into the soil in nodules on their roots, so if you leave these in the soil the brassicas that follow benefit from this and can draw on that reserve of nitrogen to produce a profusion of robust leaves. It then follows that root crops requiring less nitrogen can be planted in the next rotation after the brassicas. Also, crops such as potatoes can shade out weeds so the following year those beds should have less of a weed problem and will suit onions and carrots. Crop rotation is at the very heart of low-maintenance vegetable gardening, particularly if you are choosing to grow organically, and a bit of time spent planning will reward you for years to come.

## THE BASICS
Leave as long as possible before growing the same crop and all related crops in the same location. This avoids a buildup of pests and diseases and the partial erosion of fertility.

▶ This bed of leeks will be replaced by a crop from Group 2 (see above) next season, which in turn will be replaced with a brassica from Group 3.

# Pests and Diseases

There is nothing so heartbreaking nor infuriating in equal measure as finding that a row of vegetables you have tended and eagerly awaited eating has been decimated by pests or blighted by disease. It is a waste of time, effort, enthusiasm, and money. Preemptive measures are easier and more effective than trying to deal with problems once they have become established. This is particularly true if you are a weekend vegetable grower or community garden plot holder who can only make infrequent visits to the plot. A vast amount of damage can be done in a week, and quick fixes don't really exist—once a seedling's stem is gnawed through it is dead, as soon as rabbits find the salad leaves they are gone, and once butterfly eggs hatch into caterpillars on cabbages the outer leaves will soon look like lace. I choose not to use any chemical sprays to eradicate pests as part of my organic gardening efforts but you may feel differently. So the message is, to use a well-worn phrase, prevention is better than cure. Protect crops from the most likely diseases and pests and, where possible, avoid problems by choosing cultivars that have been shown to have disease resistance or are unappealing to pests. Going for a resistant variety is an especially good strategy if you have had a problem in previous years. The crop listings on pages 48–161 outlines the most common problems associated with each crop and ways to tackle them.

Other general strategies can help keep potential problems in check. Growing healthy, hearty plants in the best conditions you can provide will better equip them to withstand any attack. Buy plants and seeds from reputable sources and look for sturdy, stout plants that are well rooted. Don't be seduced by lavish, lush forced growth that is attractive to pests. Tidy up when you can. Never put diseased plants on the compost heap as spores and viruses will probably survive the composting process and be spread on the garden the following year. Beware gifts from other gardeners; it may seem a little ungrateful, but those spare bare-root fruit canes, rhubarb crowns, or whatever, may be the horticultural equivalent of a Trojan Horse, hiding numerous pests and viruses.

## THE BASICS

Take routine steps to protect crops.

Rotate crops to prevent reoccurring infestations.

▼ ◄ Caterpillars can cause serious damage to brassicas in the summer months.

▼ Caterpillar damage on the outer leaves of a cabbage. Despite this the head will probably be fine for eating.

## Slugs and Snails

I have tried numerous methods to deter slugs and snails. They are one of the most universally destructive forces likely to blight the vegetable garden, as they will eat entire seedlings, ravage brassicas and leave ragged holes, eat into potatoes, and demolish salad crops—the list is almost endless. The good news is that once they are large enough most plants can withstand a little damage. There are various gels and crushed minerals available that can be spread around vulnerable plants to prevent slugs and snails getting near the plants. I have tried many but have had little long-term success, as the products seem to wash away, and there is also the issue of cost to consider. Some gardeners swear by copper rings which interact with slugs' slime to produce a reaction like an electrical shock, thus deterring the slugs, but to protect everything would be a considerable investment, although the rings can be used year after year. You can attempt to reduce the population with beer traps and by constructing damp, dark slug hiding places for them so they can be collected. However, in a damp year you would have to be incredibly determined to have a significant effect.

Slugs have some natural predators such as ground beetles, although to encourage them into the garden you would have to create the same habitat that will favor slugs and snails. Shrews, frogs, and toads will also do the job if you can encourage them into your vegetable garden. I was delighted to disturb a large, gnarled toad among my salad leaves. There is a biological control available for slugs containing nematodes, which is watered into the soil when the weather starts to warm up and will attack and kill the slugs underground.

I have found simple physical barriers as effective, if not more effective than anything else. A simple plastic bottle with the bottom cut off, pushed well into the ground, will form a cloche around a seedling to protect it until it is large enough to withstand attack. Plastic rings with a down-turned lip from the garden center do the same job. Just keeping the place tidy can also help, leaving slugs and snails nowhere to hide.

One of the oddest solutions I have come across is actually feeding the marauding mollusks rotting leaves or bran to keep them off vulnerable plants. Perhaps as an emergency short-term measure it might help, but long term I think you would be boosting the population of well-fed slugs.

▲ This plastic ring with a down-turned rim protects young plants from slug damage.

## Rabbits and Deer

Rabbits and deer can cause tremendous damage to crops. In the case of deer it often seems to be inquisitiveness that causes them to uproot new plants. The only way to truly protect your garden does take an immense amount of effort—a fence that is dug into the soil to a depth of at least 10 in. (25 cm) will thwart rabbits and one 8 ft. (2.5 m) high will stop deer jumping the barrier. My garden is bounded by fields on all sides and I feel privileged to have deer, badgers, rabbits, and foxes in my garden regularly, and in most of the garden I tolerate a little damage, but the vegetable garden is a little different. Part of my plot, the original part, is fenced by very unattractive but very effective deer fencing used by the forestry industry. Made from heavy-duty plastic, nothing has as yet beaten it. The rest of my plot is open, but I try to grow really appealing vegetables inside the protection of the fence and leave crops that might not

be so tempting on the outside. Potatoes and rhubarb shouldn't be attractive to deer or rabbits since the leaves are toxic, nor should onions and leeks due to their strong smell, and the large bristly leaves of zucchinis (courgettes) and squashes should be off-putting, but I protect the young plants of all of these just in case. So far there has been little damage, but this may be more to do with the abundance of food all around!

## Mice

Mice will dig out pea and bean seeds, leaving a neat depression where you are expecting a seedling. Sowing when other food sources are scarce is more risky. The first time I planted fava beans (broad beans) to try overwintering them I could not understand why every single seed had failed, until I looked closely at the bed and discovered a beautifully accurate zigzag pattern of holes ranged over the beds—every single seed had been eaten. Now I always pin down a piece of double-thickness chicken wire tightly over the beds until the seedlings are through. You can soak peas and bean seeds in seaweed fertilizer to put rodents off the scent, or try using spiky holly leaves to protect seeds, but this seems a little haphazard to me.

▲ This fava bean (broad bean) seedling has been protected from rodents by chicken wire held down securely with large stones.

▶ A homemade chicken wire cloche will keep butterflies from laying their eggs on your cabbages, but won't stop the slugs from nibbling the leaves.

# Birds

Birds will eat soft fruit, peck holes in young brassicas, and pull onion sets out of the ground. There are two options: scare them away or cover the vulnerable crops. Moving and shiny objects will deter birds, but it pays to move them every so often. I have made my own shining aluminum spirals that twirl on thin elastic, and while I like the look of these the birds don't. I have also used old CDs and even a foil survival blanket (from an outdoor pursuits shop) cut into strips; both are very light and flutter with the slightest breeze. To protect crops I use chicken wire tunnels, very fine mesh, or fleece and these keep off butterflies, too. Plastic netting or mazes of black cotton are common solutions, but I find the number of birds liable to get tangled in the netting unacceptable.

# Aphids

Aphids include greenfly and blackfly in their prodigious numbers. They suck the sap of plants, slightly weakening them, but the main problem is that they can spread disease. Preparing salad leaves littered with greenfly is tedious and off-putting. Covering salad crops with a floating layer of fleece solves this problem, and pinching the tips out of broad bean plants will slow down the blackfly that almost inevitably infest them. I have also dislodged blackfly from artichoke plants with a strong, well-aimed jet of water. As a group these are perhaps the most common pests, and the best way to keep them in check is to encourage their natural predators, which are ladybugs, lacewings, and hoverflies and their larvae. All should be part of a healthily biodiverse garden, but they can be encouraged by companion planting and providing special boxes for overwintering.

Pesticides are available for edible crops, although their number is becoming ever more limited. I choose not to use them but if you do, carefully read the manufacturer's information and apply them only to the crops recommended, respecting the number of days before harvest restrictions. It is a personal choice but I would rather rely on all the other measures listed here to protect my crops and tolerate a little damage than use synthetic pesticides on plants I give my family to eat.

▲ Anything reflective and mobile is likely to deter birds, and these spirals on elastic will twirl in the slightest breeze.

# Caterpillars

Butterflies are one of the joys of the garden in summer, and in most parts of the garden they are a welcome visitor, with many of us planting nectar-rich plants to encourage them. Sadly they don't stay in the flower garden and the caterpillars of a few species can wreck brassicas. The biggest problem is the cabbage white, which lays its eggs on the brassicas' leaves where they hatch into caterpillars who then eat the cabbages until the leaves look like dirty green lace. The easiest solution is to prevent the butterflies getting to the plants using homespun chicken wire cloches or sheets of insect-proof mesh.

# Companion Planting

Growing a combination of plants together for the benefits they bestow upon each other is known as companion planting. Harnessing these qualities keeps the garden healthy and productive. There are a number of specific ways that growing different plants in combination can make life on the vegetable plot easier. In general growing a range of plants of different types, such as flowering plants and herbs, among the vegetables to edge beds or between the rows will improve the biodiversity of the garden, keep pests from easily locating their prey, and also attract beneficial insects. Adding flowering plants and herbs also contributes a burst of welcome color and scent to the garden, and if I can I use companion plants that are edible too, such as nasturtiums and calendula, so they really earn their keep.

Attracting beneficial insects into the vegetable patch, those that will feast on the pests that inhabit the vegetable garden, is another very worthwhile method to keep potential problems with pests under control. Lacewings, hoverflies, and ladybugs will consume vast numbers of aphids and caterpillars, while parasitic wasps will lay their eggs into the pests, their larvae eating the host once it hatches. The poached eggplant, calendula, and the California poppy will all attract beneficial insects, and I tend to use calendula because the petals of the punchy, orange flowers are great sprinkled over a crisp green salad. Other flowers have the ability to repel pests: pungent marigolds will repel whitefly and chives will repel aphids. The leaves of fresh chives can be snipped up and used to give an onion kick to plenty of dishes. While pretty, purple chive flowers and peppery nasturtium flowers are another fantastic way to give a salad a touch of pizzazz, and the leaves have a taste that is similar to cress. So again, these companion plants really earn their place in the garden. I grow trailing, vibrantly colored nasturtiums through my squashes and pumpkins where the competition will do no harm, creating a wonderful visual feast. Both nasturtiums and marigolds will contribute to the cacophony of scents that will keep pests guessing. Nasturtiums can also be used as a "fall guy" to take the hit of blackfly that might otherwise blight fava beans (broad beans), although this does of course make them much less appetizing! Growing spring onions with carrots to mask the scent of the carrots from the carrot root fly is another example of companion planting, a simple strategy that really works.

One plant making the soil more fertile for another is an alternative meaning of companion planting. Peas and beans fix nitrogen in the soil, a characteristic used in traditional crop rotation schemes (see page 182), but the crops could be combined from the outset, growing brassicas, sweet corn, sweet peas, or cucumbers in the same area.

Having a diversity of nectar-rich flowers also has the advantage of encouraging pollinating insects into the plot, ensuring crops such as peas and beans are well pollinated. A word of caution, these companion plants are performing a valuable service but they are also occupying space and taking up nutrients and water from the soil. If they grow too strongly they might even crowd out the crops you are trying to protect. I once made the mistake of edging all my long beds with large nasturtiums. It soon became clear that they were very happy as they grew very quickly, outperforming the crops in the beds and swamping them, so much so that they all had to be removed.

## THE BASICS

Companion planting uses the characteristics of one plant to benefit another or to encourage beneficial insects.

Growing a variety of plants will improve biodiversity and make the vegetable garden more healthy and productive.

Useful companion plants are nasturtiums, calendula, poached eggplant, and marigolds.

▶ Planted in spring, the nasturtiums and calendula that form the mainstay of my companion planting are still going strong in late autumn.

# Growing in Containers

Just about anything will grow in a container if it is lavished with enough care and attention. A range of attractive containers can transform even a small balcony, terrace, or courtyard into a pretty and productive garden. Crops in pots are far more reliant on the gardener for all their needs as the soil in containers can dry out quickly and the nutrients in the soil soon deplete. So feeding and watering are very important—most containers will need watering twice a day in the hottest part of the year to ensure a good crop. A drip feed irrigation system is a simple solution that will ensure an adequate supply of water even if you are away for a few days, and an occasional liquid feed from a watering can should keep nutrient levels high. Mulching the tops of the pots with garden compost, pebbles, or a landscape fabric can help reduce moisture loss. The good news is that once the plants are in the pots and the watering and feeding is taken care of there isn't a great deal more to do, except keep watch for pests and diseases. It pays to have a few companion plants in pots, too—nasturtiums, marigolds, and calendula are my favorites—to keep aphids away and encourage pollinators.

Compact varieties are best suited to growing in containers and most seed catalogs have a number of miniature cultivars developed for growing in pots and window boxes. There is no reason, however, why you shouldn't grow runner beans or raspberries up cane obelisks, or a worthwhile crop of early potatoes, ruby chard, zucchinis (courgettes), ballerina fruit trees, or dwarf fava beans (broad beans) alongside the more obvious tomatoes, strawberries, and salad leaves. Growing in pots can even make life easier if you are trying to grow something like blueberries which need an acid soil, if you don't have one. They will thrive in a container filled with good-quality ericaceous (acidic) compost.

Annual crops can be grown in multi-purpose compost and will need feeding about a month to six weeks after planting. For very hungry crops such as runner beans and zucchinis (courgettes), the multi-purpose compost could be beefed up with some garden compost or well-rotted manure if you have it. At the end of the season the compost will be spent and can be tossed on the compost heap or used as a mulch, although, if you are growing plants that mature quickly,

the pots can be replanted in that season but with a different crop.

Anything that will be in its pot for a long period, such as fruit trees, needs a different treatment; use the largest pot reasonable for the plant and start by putting something weighty, such as a few bricks, in the base of the pot to make it less likely to blow over in the wind. Use a loam-based compost mixed with multi-purpose compost and a few handfuls of grit—this mix holds onto nutrients and water well and won't become compacted. If you live in a cold area it may be necessary to wrap permanent pots in layers of bubble wrap or bring the pots inside in the winter to prevent the compost and roots from freezing.

## THE BASICS

Crops grown in containers are more dependent on the gardener.

Regular feeding and watering is essential.

Almost anything can be grown in a pot if the pot is large enough.

**Top left** Cherry tomatoes are the ideal subjects for container growing. Keep them watered and fed and grow in a warm spot.

**Top right** Almost anything that will hold a good quantity of compost can be used as a container. This inexpensive bucket is practical and looks great.

**Bottom left** Pea plants are ideal for container growing, and tips of young plants can be used in summer salads.

**Bottom right** With water and regular feeding, strawberries will do well in pretty much any container. Here they are being grown in a wine box.

# Calendar

It would be blissfully reassuring to have absolute dates given for the best time to plant each crop, a hard and fast immutable timetable for when the air and soil temperature will be just right. However, in reality this is just not possible. Temperatures and conditions vary wildly from area to area at the same time of year, and in the same area from one year to the next. The best you can do is offer a rule of thumb and employ a bit of common sense. In the following list I've divided tasks by season and this should be used as a guide to help you plan your plot and draw up your own plan for repeat sowing. However, bear in mind that this is flexible and can be adapted. For example, just because it is possible to sow carrots from early spring to late summer you don't have to, just plan to sow as many times as you need to.

## Spring

This is probably the most exciting and busiest time of the year in the garden, and as the days become longer and warmer I am always glad of the excuse to spend time outside. There is of course that feeling of panic that I will never be ready, the beds will not be cleared and mulched in good time for planting, the supports in place for my bean plants, and there are always those few persistent weeds to tackle. Getting the garden ready to go in late winter and early spring is the most concentrated period of effort in the garden, and is the only period when I actually set aside time to garden (a real luxury, as usually tasks have to be shoehorned in around everything else). It seems that earmarking

a glorious couple of half days when the weather is fine means I can get everything shipshape, the beds mulched and off to a great start. This saves masses of time later, and when I only have 15 minutes to pop out and get the latest plants to arrive in the ground, everything is ready. I also take heart from knowing that if I was growing everything from seed I would be spending hours coaxing them to germinate, tending trays and trays of young seedlings, and worrying about the temperature of a greenhouse at this time of year. But, as it is, someone else does all this for me and I am delivered perfect young plants at just the right time of year.

### Early Spring
**Sow directly into the soil**
Fava beans (broad beans)
Carrots
Jerusalem artichokes
Potatoes
Radishes
Peas
Spring onions
Shallots
Nasturtiums and calendula

**Plant**
Summer and autumn cabbages
Artichokes
Onion sets
Early potatoes
Container-grown fruit bushes
**Other tasks and tips**
- The annual mulch! Mulch the whole growing area and around all perennials with garden compost, except for the bed that is to be sown with carrots.

- If you have ordered asparagus crowns, create a bed ready for their arrival (see pages 97–99).
- Clear away any remaining plant debris and weed thoroughly.
- Collect (or buy) pea sticks.
- Put up runner bean supports.
- Chit potatoes.
- Prune fruit bushes.
- Tidy the strawberry bed and mulch with straw.

### Late Spring

**Sow directly into the soil**

Carrots
Zucchini (courgettes) and summer squash (marrows)
Lettuce
Onion sets
Peas
Potatoes
Radishes
Runner beans
Salad leaves

**Plant**

Asparagus crowns
Celeriac
Cabbage
Leeks
Perpetual spinach
Swiss chard
Artichokes
Zucchini (courgettes)

**Other tasks and tips**

- Pinch out the tips of fava bean (broad bean) plants to prevent blackfly from infesting them.
- Hoe around onions and carrots.
- Earth up potatoes if you are not using one of the low-maintenance methods described on pages 73–77.
- Have some fleece handy to sling over young plants to protect them from late frosts.

# Summer

With most of the groundwork done, now is the time to keep on top of weeds, water where necessary, and start reaping the rewards of your work by enjoying some of your lovely homegrown vegetables. All of the plants in your beds should be bursting with life and growing rapidly until the garden looks as though it may split at the seams.

### Early Summer

**Sow directly into the soil**

Beets (beetroot)
Borlotti beans
Carrots
Green beans (French beans)
Radishes
Peas
Runner beans
Salad leaves
Spring onions
Sweet corn

**Plant**

Zucchini (courgettes) and summer squash (marrows)
Pumpkins and squashes
Sweet corn
Tomatoes
Peppers and chillies
Eggplants (aubergines)

**Other tasks and tips**

- Hoe around onions and carrots.
- Mulch where you can, a great way to use up grass cuttings.

### Late Summer

**Sow directly into the soil**

Salad leaves
Winter salad leaf mixes containing Pak choi, Mizuna, Mustard spinach, and Radicchio
Radishes
Winter-hardy spring onions

**Plant**

Cabbages

**Other tasks and tips**

- Some zucchini (courgette) leaves will probably be affected by mildew, a white powdery-looking substance on the leaves. It is almost inevitable so don't panic, simply remove the affected leaves and destroy them.
- Hoe and mulch to keep weeds under control.

# Autumn

Your garden tasks become a great deal more relaxed in the autumn. This is the season when many plants will still be giving a good harvest, brightly colored squashes and pumpkins come into their own, and the vegetable patch begins to soften a little. All of the bright green lushness and vigor of the summer's rapid growth fades a little and mellows.

### Early Autumn
**Sow directly into the soil**
Winter salad leaves
**Plant**
Spring cabbages
**Other tasks and tips**
- Plant rhubarb, although plants will normally be available in spring as well.
- Protect winter salad leaves with a fleece if necessary.

### Late Autumn
**Sow directly into the soil**
Fava beans (broad beans)
Garlic
Shallots
**Plant**
Bare-root fruit bushes
Rhubarb
Strawberries

### Other tasks and tips
- Collect leaves for making leaf mold.
- Prune blackberries.
- Protect celeriac and globe artichoke crowns with a mulch of straw or a layer of fleece.

# Winter

If you have planned well and have a gentle climate, there will still be crops to harvest through even the bleakest months. It always feels like a major triumph when nature has essentially shut up shop for the winter to go out and pull a few leeks or look at the fresh green shoots of autumn-sown garlic standing bravely through a covering of snow.

### Early Winter
**Sow directly into the soil**
Fava beans (broad beans)
**Plant**
Garlic
Onions
Shallots
**Other tasks and tips**
- Give the vegetable garden a good tidy up.
- Construct new beds ready for spring planting.

### Late Winter
**Sow**
Fava beans (broad beans)
**Plant**
Jerusalem artichokes
Shallots
Onions
Garlic

### Other tasks
- Put an upturned trash can, chimney pot, or purpose-made forcing pot on any rhubarb you want to force.
- Make your "to grow" list and order your plants.

# PART V

# Gardening the Low-Maintenance Way

Beyond the actual cultivation of the soil and the tending of plants, there are plenty of other activities that go into making a great vegetable garden. Some, such as compost-making, are absolutely essential, while others are just pure fun. The low-maintenance vegetable garden doesn't need to be all work and no play. Be it by choice or necessity, choosing to grow your own the low-maintenance way doesn't mean that your garden can't be beautiful or a pleasurable place to spend time. On the following pages you will find some tips that will make your vegetable garden both functional and enjoyable, and enjoyment is really what gardening is all about.

# Compost Made Easy

Making compost is a fundamental part of any vegetable gardening project, but especially in the no-dig plot (see page 166). Garden compost is one of the most valuable commodities in the vegetable plot for improving the soil and providing replenishing levels of nutrients in the soil, and making it isn't hard. For the most part it is a by-product of the gardening process, costs nothing, and takes very little work to achieve acceptable results. Garden compost improves the soil's ability to hold moisture and at the same time helps create air pockets in the soil, allowing water to work its way through the soil, thus helping to create a good medium for healthy root growth while encouraging biodiversity in the soil. Not only is garden compost a readily available and inexpensive way to improve the soil's fertility, but it is also very effective, providing a whole array of nutrients and trace elements. In a warm summer a "hot" heap (see page 200) can produce usable compost in just three to four months.

Just one last word on what to expect: your homemade compost may be lumpy, coarse, and quite unlike anything you might buy or pictures you may have seen in books, and it is likely it will contain some partially rotted material that can be put back into the bin. So long as the composting process has taken place, it is fine and will do wonders for your soil.

## What to Compost

- Green garden waste (but not any growth showing signs of disease as this may well survive the composting process and spread across your plot as you spread the compost).
- Kitchen waste (excluding cooked food waste, animal or dairy products).
- Cut grass.
- Leaves (although these are better used as leaf mold, see page 201).
- Annual weeds and nettle tops (but no flower heads).
- Tea bags and coffee grounds.
- Shredded woody prunings (left unshredded they will take too long to rot down).
- Animal manure.
- Egg boxes, newspaper, and unglazed cardboard.

## What Not to Compost

- Diseased vegetation, as this may do more harm than good to your vegetable plot if the disease survives the composting process and is then spread around your plot.
- Weeds that have gone to seed or the roots of perennial weeds such as bindweed, creeping buttercup, or ground elder. The likelihood is that these will not be killed during the composting process, and as you spread your compost you will be planting weeds. To safely add these to the heap put them into a sealed black plastic sack or bucket of water for a couple of months, and only add them to the heap when they have become an unrecognizable sludge.
- Animal feces.

## THE BASICS

Add a good balance of lush green waste and coarser brown waste to the heap in alternating layers.

Never add too much of one thing in a single layer—no more than 6 in. (15 cm).

Keep the heap warm by covering it.

Retain moisture levels by covering the compost, and add more soft green waste if it seems too dry.

If the heap seems too wet, mix scrunched-up newspaper or coarse waste and add a rain-proof cover.

# Which Compost Bin?

The type of compost bin you choose will depend on space and budget.

### Plastic Bins

If you have a pocket-sized patch, then a couple of the plastic composting bins available from garden centers should fit the bill. These are light, their fabric is maintenance free, and can be easily moved if needed. Choose bins at least 44 gallons (200 liters) in volume as smaller bins are likely to make the composting process less efficient, and if possible select a bin with a hatch near the base so compost that is ready can be easily removed from the heap.

### Wooden Bins

If you have space and economy is not a priority, then large purpose-made wooden bins in various styles are available, and again you will need at least two bins so that one can be filled while the other is working. A thrifty option is to put together a bin from old pallets, either wired together or wired to posts on three sides and with an opening front to make removing the finished compost easy. Add a tarpaulin covering to conserve heat and moisture.

### Open Heap

My first attempts at making compost were open heaps, simply heaping waste up in a hidden corner, turning it occasionally and waiting, or burrowing in to find some compost ready for use. There is nothing wrong with this method so long as you periodically turn the edges into the center. It is simple and there are no structures to buy or build, but the frequent turning of the heap is backbreaking work and the rotting process takes a very long time, so I really wouldn't recommend it.

▲ This compost bin constructed from old pallets is a lovely piece of pragmatic recycling and will make compost just as well as fancier models at a fraction of the cost.

▲ Perhaps the ultimate in home compost, a three-bin system allows for one bin to be filled while another is maturing and one is in use—ideal in a large plot.

## Adding Material to Your Heap

The key to good compost is to build your heap in layers of material with different characteristics, with no single layer being too thick. Luckily this normally happens as a matter of course as the heap grows out of the varied activities around the garden. This is where it can all begin to sound like a chemistry lesson, with the ideal heap being one consisting of equal amounts of nitrogen-rich and carbon-rich material, but if you think of it in terms of a good balance between green material (grass clippings, plant waste, and peelings) providing nitrogen and brown material (coarser things like woody plant remains, dead leaves, and newspaper) providing carbon, it becomes simpler. The ideal is to follow a green layer with a brown layer, to keep the heap's structure open, allowing air and water to permeate the heap. The greatest likelihood is that you will have too much green material, especially from grass clippings—a dense layer of grass clippings will form a black slime rather than wholesome compost, so keep a pile of cardboard, straw, or scrunched-up newspapers handy and add some of this every time you have an overabundance of green material. Chopping or cutting the material on the heap into small pieces makes decomposition faster as it gives the microbes that cause decomposition more surface area to get stuck into.

## Problems Solved

If a heap is becoming slimy, smelly, and sludgy rather than decomposing properly, it is too wet and there is insufficient air in the heap. Mix the contents of the bin with chopped straw, scrunched-up newspaper, or coarser brown waste, ensure the bottom layer of the bin allows drainage, and cover the bin with a tarpaulin to keep the rain out.

If the material heap is not decomposing it is probably because the heap is too dry. The best solution is to turn the heap out and mix in plenty of soft green waste and return it to the bin. If this isn't available, watering the heap is a possibility and adding a covering to keep the moisture in.

## Making a Hot Heap

If you want compost in a hurry, building a hot heap can transform waste into compost, sometimes in as little as three months, but the longer you leave the compost the better it will be. A compost bin is filled in one hit rather than a little at a time, carefully alternating 6 in. (15 cm) layers of greens and browns and using shredded newspaper or chopped straw, and covering to keep in moisture and heat.

## Using a Worm Bin

Hungry brandling worms will munch their way through about their own body weight in kitchen waste per day to produce very rich compost and a liquid feed. This way more kitchen waste can be recycled than can be added to a standard compost heap. Purpose-made worm bins are available and worms can be bought by mail order. The bins need to be well sealed to avoid vermin, and everything except onion and citrus fruit waste can be added for recycling by the wonderful worms. Waste can be added daily and the liquid requires draining off regularly to avoid the bin flooding.

# Leaf Mold

Most of us have some leaves to clear from lawns, paths, and patios in the autumn. It amazes me how many people take the trouble to collect the leaves and then burn them rather than converting them into one of the best soil conditioners available, which is no more effort, in fact possibly less effort, than coaxing a damp bonfire into life. If you have very few leaves, they can be added to the general compost heap but they take a long time to rot down.

Leaf mold is described as a soil conditioner as it is low in nutrients and does not really feed the soil but rather improves the soil structure. Whether you have a heavy or light soil, leaf mold's beautifully crumbly texture will open up the structure of dense, claggy soils and help light, free-draining soils to retain water. It can be put on the garden at any time of the year and can be used in thick layers to suppress weeds.

Making leaf mold couldn't be easier: simply gather the fallen leaves and dump them into black plastic sacks, tie the tops of the bags, and pierce a few holes in the sacks. They can then be stacked in an unobtrusive spot. The leaves will take at least a year to rot down, some perhaps two years, but storing the leaf mold for longer will give it a finer texture. Some mechanical leaf collectors chop the leaves as they vacuum them up, and this will speed up the process. If you have the time and want to do the collecting task twice, you can gather the fallen leaves in a pile and run over them with the lawn mower to the same effect. To be honest, piling them in a black sack and waiting a bit longer is easier, neater, and much less effort.

If you have the space you could invest in constructing a leaf mold bin—this is simply a length of chicken wire stretched around some posts that have been driven into the ground to form a large basket. The fallen leaves are put in the resulting bin and left to rot in the same way.

## THE BASICS

A great soil conditioner and mulch.

Collect fallen leaves in the autumn and leave them to rot in black sacks with holes or a chicken-wire bin for at least a year.

◀ Made in about an hour, a simple post and wire bin is the perfect way to make leaf mold on a large scale if you have the space.

# The Tools You Really Need

There is a plethora of gardening tools available, some unchanged for centuries, others the latest shiny garden gadgets boasting some spectacular and irresistible advantages. But only a few simple tools are required to maintain the average no-dig plot. The fewer tools you accumulate, the easier they are to look after and store. If your budget allows, it is worth investing in well-made tools from the outset as they will give years of good service. Failing this, secondhand tools from junk shops can offer great value if they are sound, and they often have a wonderful mellow glow resulting from hours of toil in the garden. When buying secondhand tools, always look at wooden handles carefully, especially where they meet the metal implement, checking for any signs of rot or woodworm. Plastic handles are generally lighter and more durable, though not as nice to work with.

When choosing any tool, take the opportunity to check the weight and size are right for you. Tools that are too heavy or the wrong size make any task harder work.

## Trowel

A simple hand trowel is a versatile tool used for weeding, planting, harvesting, and small-scale cultivation. Here I make an exception to the assertion that you should "buy the best you can afford" as in my experience trowels are the most frequently lost tools, turning up months or years later in the compost heap or hidden by foliage in the corner of a bed. Even applying a coat of fluorescent paint to the handles hasn't lessened the number I lose, so I have two inexpensive trowels just in case.

## Small Border Fork

Used for digging out compost and applying mulch to beds.

## Spade or Long-Handled Spade

Used for digging out compost and applying mulch to beds.

## Wheelbarrow

Essential for transporting everything around the garden.

## Plastic Tub

These flexible tubs have a myriad of uses, from collecting weeds and debris generated in the tidying up process to being bent inward and used like a jug to dispense free-flowing mulches, such as mushroom compost, around plants.

## String Line

If you are using small beds, you will probably be able to get pretty good lines by eye or by using a cane, but longer rows will probably require a string line to guide you. Make your own with a length of brightly colored, durable twine and a couple of lengths of dowel.

## Hoe

There are two kinds of hoe: the Dutch hoe and the draw hoe. Choosing which one to use is really a matter of personal preference; both are used for weeding and uprooting or severing seedlings before they become established and will fit neatly between rows of veg. You really only need one—if you have no preference, go for the Dutch hoe.

## Watering Can

Metal or plastic cans are available. Plastic cans are lighter and less expensive and often come with measurements marked on the side to help with applying liquid fertilizers that need diluting. Remember that you will be carrying the can when full, so while larger cans may look like time-savers they may also be backbreakers.

## Pruners (Secateurs)

These are needed for pruning, tidying up plant material, and harvesting.

## Old Kitchen Knife

Special garden knives are available, but an old kitchen knife or pen knife will work just as well for jobs like cutting twine, harvesting crops such as zucchinis (courgettes), and cutting the leaves from rhubarb.

Having your most-used tools and materials in a handy trug or basket can save much hunting around in the shed.

### Gloves

Essential for taking on thorny pruning and spiky weeds, thick protective gloves can be leather or heavy rubber. Thinner rubber or latex gloves work better for jobs where some precision is required. Often gloves intended for use in the building trade or in the kitchen work just as well in the garden and tend to be less expensive.

### Dibble (Dibber)

Used to make small holes in the soil for planting large seeds, making seed furrows and transplanting leeks and other plants. Traditionally, the broken handle of a fork or spade was cut down and rounded to make a functional dibble, but a length of broom handle or dowel rod will suffice. You could add markings to indicate measurements to take the guesswork out of planting depths.

## Keeping Tools Handy

If you only have 15 minutes to spend in the vegetable garden, the most frustrating and wasteful thing is to spend five of those precious minutes looking for the tools or bits and pieces you need. The easiest way around this is to have a handy toolbox, for want of a better name, kept just by the back door, in the shed, or anywhere dry en route to the vegetable patch. This might be a plastic tray, cloth bag, or as in my case a beech trug. This can be picked up on your way to the garden and will hold everything you may need; my suggested list of indispensable items to include is:
- Trowel
- Pruners (secateurs)
- Knife
- Twine
- Labels
- Waterproof marker
- Dibble (dibber)
- Gloves

## Other Essentials

Having some or all of the materials below to hand will make it simple to protect vulnerable crops from insect pests and frosts as soon as needed.

### Fleece

Horticultural fleece is an incredibly useful white fabric. It can be used as a floating mulch, protecting plants from insect pests and frost, or used to warm up the soil early in spring. It gets a little grubby but will last several seasons.

### Chicken Wire

Can be pinned to the soil to keep rodents away from pea and bean seeds or bent into arched tunnels to keep birds and butterflies off brassicas.

### Insect-Proof Mesh

Used to protect crops from even the smallest insect pest. Reasonably expensive but can be reused and has the advantage of allowing more air to circulate than fleece.

### Plastic Bottles

Make individual cloches for small seedlings to protect them from slugs.

### Seed Compost

For planting small seeds.

Invaluable for planting seeds, leeks, and onion sets, a calibrated dibble is a garden essential.

# Looking Good

Creating a glorious vegetable garden with a few simple home comforts that looks good even when slightly neglected works wonders in getting the work done—it is not a time-saver, it's a motivator. Toiling in a beautiful garden makes tending the vegetables more enjoyable and adds to the sense of achievement. For few this may not be an issue, but just walking into the vegetable plot can be an uplifting experience, making it a great place to spend time. There are not many people who would feel elated at walking into an unappealing jumble that is hard to work in, even if the harvest is good. How you create your own personal vegetable garden heaven is an individual choice and it need not take much investment of time or money but just a little thought. You may only need a garden that looks well tended, with a bench for that well-deserved break, or you could add a few objet trouvé, or settle for making the garden essentials, such as obelisks and labels, decorative. From a rural idyll with hazel rods for beans to spiral up and battered metal watering cans, to a garden with a modern twist with clean lines and stainless steel raised beds, there are plenty of styles to choose from. Keeping the vegetable patch looking good is even more important if it is on view from the house, within the garden or located at the front of the house. Whichever, the prime function of the vegetable patch is to grow tasty crops, and what I am suggesting is simply adding a little value—making tending your plot more pleasurable and developing your own personal slice of vegetable garden paradise will guarantee you want to spend time there.

▲ In a predominantly green bed the vibrant colors of the sweet peas are a welcome treat.

◀ Among the flowers for cutting, the sweet corn holds its own as an ornamental.

▶ The vegetable garden can be practical as well as appealing, and this mirrored gazing ball helps to create a sense of tranquility.

# Pretty Planting

Keeping plants in neat rows has plenty of advantages for making garden maintenance simple, but there is no reason why those rows or blocks cannot be combined in a way that sets up an attractive tapestry of colors and textures. Common sense has to prevail and crop rotation considered, yet there are plenty of ways to have some fun and create a visual feast, as well as growing one. Lettuces are an obvious example and the drama and fussiness of a frilly red variety such as 'Sentry' next to the glistening green of an upright form such as 'Pinokkio' set in alternate blocks or rows has real visual impact.

Rows of carrots and onions with their contrasting feathery slender foliage look appealing and will confuse the carrot fly, too. If you are growing in small beds, some plants are natural "edgers"—perpetual spinach is a tidy grower and will provide a leafy green frame for a bed all year round, as will chives or parsley. Spring onions, radishes, or beets (beetroot) are more transient but will do the job.

The vibrant flowers of companion plants are almost a relief among the predominantly leafy greenness and can be used to add a bit of zing to the plot. Shockingly orange calendula alongside red cabbages or 'Black Tuscany' kale is an eye-catching combination, as are the flowers of brilliant red nasturtiums among the blue-green stems of leeks. Using colorful cultivars, such as chard 'Northern Lights' or Green bean (French bean) 'Cobra' with its pretty lilac flowers or the scarlet-daubed pods of borlotti beans, all contribute to making the vegetable garden a more colorful and interesting place.

**As these red cabbages grow, the orange calendula will look stunning against them.**

**The contrasting leaf colors and forms of these lettuce make a striking pattern.**

**A single row of spring onions is a neat way to edge a bed.**

# Gaining Height

All vegetable plots need some vertical structures, if only to support beans, sweet peas, and cucumbers. These offer the chance to quite literally add a new dimension to the design of the garden and are a space-saving way to grow. Simple cane tunnels work, but there are plenty of other options—climbers can be grown over arches or tunnels spanning paths or gateways, or up obelisks, which works well in formal gardens where they can be placed symmetrically. Impressive lumber or willow obelisks are available to buy, but you could try something more homespun: old tools, past their best, tied together at the top and pushed into the ground to make an apt, quirky obelisk or simple pieces of planed lumber, painted and tied at the top, add height and vibrant color. These are temporary, low-cost features, so you can use your imagination and have a bit of fun. As well as temporary obelisks I use permanent rope structures to support climbers in my garden—made from a synthetic hemp lookalike, they are practical and will last for years.

Half-standard bay or gooseberries or ballerina fruit trees all make striking vertical punctuations. Bays instantly evoke traditional formality, while gooseberries are a little more wayward with a loose twiggy topknot. Ballerina fruit trees grow a single stem straight up to about 6 ½ ft. (2 m) and require no pruning. They are productive, pretty, and space-savers, producing blossom and fruit, and the space beneath them can be planted.

Practical supports, such as this one for cucumbers, can add a visual dimension to the garden.

Standard bays and formal teepees give this pretty garden height and structure.

# Flowers for Picking

Although I have many large and lavishly planted beds of perennials, I can seldom bring myself to cut a single bloom for the house. So in the first expansion of my kitchen garden, I was keen to include an area for cut flowers. I had always grown sweet peas (a personal vegetable plot essential) but I added dahlias, crocosmia, and gladioli—all flowers I would be unlikely to use in the flower garden—in vibrant colors specifically for cutting. It proved maintenance free beyond applying some mulch, and it was nice to be able to take bunches of flowers from the garden when visiting friends and have plenty of blooms for the house. In truth, however, they made the kitchen garden look so good I still begrudged cutting them. Avoid using any invasive perennials though, as these may be detrimental to your vegetables.

## Sweet Peas

I call these a vegetable garden essential. Grown up simple supports or even among the runner beans, the delicate sweet pea will fill the garden with the most delicious fragrance—"the smell of summer" as my daughter calls it. On a practical level sweet peas will encourage pollinators into the garden, but I grow them for their irresistible, delicate flowers and scent. They are the one flower where cutting is not a problem—in fact it is essential to keep the plants producing more blooms. They thrive in the rich soil of the no-dig garden and come in an array of colors. I buy named varieties as small plants in mid-spring, experimenting with different mixes of colors. A small bunch will fill a room with fragrance.

Clockwise from left: Gladiolus 'Green Goddess' and red dahlia, dahlia 'Fireball,' crocosmia 'Walberton Yellow,' dahlia 'Don Hill.'

## Dahlias

Commonly grown as a cut flower due to the length of time they stay looking good once cut, dahlias come in an almost infinite array of forms, colors, and sizes. From large rounded pompoms to spiky cactus, or simple daisy-flowered types, garish pinks and yellows to more sophisticated dark, rich mahoganies and lime greens. They enjoy rich soil and are fairly trouble-free. They are grown from tubers planted in early spring, and in warm areas can be left in the ground over winter. In cold areas the tubers need to be lifted in autumn and replanted the following year.

## Crocosmia

Very easy to grow, reliably producing the freshest green spikes of new leaves in spring and flowers in mid- to late summer. They come in a range of oranges, reds, and yellows; the pretty flowers last well when cut and the seed heads are attractive, too.

## Gladioli

Planted as bulbs, gladioli are stately flowers with sword-shaped leaves and rigid spikes of trumpet flowers. They come in a whole range of magnificent colors, from almost black to lime green, as well as a whole range of insipid colors that are not as appealing.

▲ A length of wood with a coat of paint makes a practical and attractive label.

▶ Always keen to recycle, bright plastic bottles make quirky labels and add a splash of color.

# Making Necessities Nicer

There are plenty of opportunities to take the mundane areas of gardening and make them more interesting, contributing to a plot to be proud of, and this doesn't have to involve great expense. Labels are an essential and most standard plastic labels are too small, soon getting lost under an abundance of foliage. Sturdy chunks of planed wood with a lick of bright wood stain are far more practical and striking. Write the plant names on with waterproof marker, and the labels will last for years. I have also recycled brightly colored plastic bottles, which really stand out.

Bird-scarers offer the chance to add a bit of creativity, too. I cut a sheet of mirror-finish aluminum into strips and curled them to form spirals, and while I love the sparkle and movement, the birds stayed away. Carefully strung lines of CDs have the same effect. A scarecrow makes a real statement on the plot and there is plenty of room for imagination in the choice of look, though I am unconvinced of their long-term efficiency!

I am partially ashamed to admit it but I even chose my wonderful watering can as much for its good looks as its practicality—a giant old aluminum can that looks good wherever it is left in the garden. Like my grubby ancient line, given to me by my father, or the trug I keep my tools in that belonged to my grandfather, they are just a pleasure to use and have around. Ornamental cloches, frames, and forcing jars are all available if you want to splurge. If this kind of thing is not important to you, then just get on with growing good vegetables, but for me (and I guess many others) it all adds up to a much more rewarding experience.

Cut from a sheet of mirrored metal and bent by hand, this bird deterrent looks better than most.

# When the Work Is Done

Every vegetable garden should have at least one seat, a place to enjoy a deserved break, survey your achievements, and plan the next session's chores. Although there are plenty of other places to sit in my garden, I still find I often choose to sit in the vegetable garden. Chunky, robust natural furniture probably sits best in most vegetable gardens, except the breathtaking contemporary gardens with stark metal beds. Keep in mind that those sitting on the benches are likely to be fairly muddy. I have some bright deck chairs, but the canvas soon becomes dirty.

One of the nicest possible things in a very decorative vegetable garden is to have space for eating outside or a barbecue in the garden—a place to enjoy the food where it is growing, the freshest food you can get. A simple barbecue would do. I have a very basic outdoor kitchen with an open fireplace that doubles as a barbecue and a pizza oven a few steps away from my vegetable garden. The food is literally plucked from the plant and enjoyed—a real celebration of the pleasure, wonder, and terrific tastes of growing your own.

▲ It is hard to beat an old-fashioned deck chair for relaxing outside in the vegetable plot, but they can get dirty.

◄ The gentle sway of a swing seat adds an extra soothing element to a relaxing break from work.

► Just a few steps away from my vegetable patch this basic outdoor kitchen with a stone oven and chunky oak worktops is a fitting place to prepare and cook vegetables fresh from the garden, and this chair is great to retreat to when the work is done.

# Jargon Buster

**biennial**
Planted one year to flower and fruit the next.

**bolting**
Prematurely producing flowers, undesirable in plants like lettuces and onions that are normally harvested before they flower. Bolting can be caused by lack of water or changes in temperature.

**broadcast**
To sprinkle seed over the soil rather than in rows.

**catch crop**
A quickly growing crop grown between slower-growing main crops.

**companion planting**
Grouping plants together so that one confers a benefit on the other, normally in dealing with pests.

**crown**
The root system of the plant, such as rhubarb, or the central part of the root system where shoots develop.

**earthing up**
Drawing soil up around the stems of plants to partially bury them. Usually done with a hoe and most often associated with potatoes.

**F1 hybrid**
A first generation cross between two pure strains. The crop produced is very consistent, but the plants do not come true from seed.

**fine tilth**
A layer of soil cultivated so it has a uniform texture of fine crumbs, ideal for planting small seeds.

**fleece**
Horticultural fleece is a white fabric, usually bought off the roll at garden centers. It is used to protect plants from frost and insect pests.

**forcing**
Encouraging rhubarb or sea kale to produce shoots earlier than they might otherwise do by inverting a large container over them to exclude light.

**forking**
Used of carrots and root vegetables to describe a division of the taproot, usually caused by growing them in recently manured ground.

**green manure**
A crop grown to be dug into the soil to improve fertility.

**harden off**
To slowly acclimatize plants to outside conditions when they have been grown inside.

**heritage variety**
Usually a term used by seed companies to describe cultivars that have been in cultivation for many years.

**leaf mold**
A great soil conditioner made from decomposed leaves.

**lime**
Added to acid soil to increase the pH, that is to make it more alkaline to suit crops like brassicas.

**landscape fabric (membrane)**
Weed-suppressing landscape fabric, or membrane, lets water through but prevents weeds growing. Used under gravel or bark-chip paths.

**main crop**
A crop that will take most of the growing season to mature and which occupies most of the bed in which it is planted.

**mulch**
Any substance that is used to cover the soil, to improve the soil, inhibit weed growth, or retain moisture.

**mushroom compost**
A waste product of the mushroom-growing industry. Good for bulking up soils and improving water retention, but it does not add nutrition.

## NPK
The chemical symbols for the major nutrients plants require. N is nitrogen that builds leaves, P is phosphorus that builds roots, and K is potassium, sometimes referred to as potash, which builds fruits and flowers.

## nitrogen fixing
This term refers to the process by which plants like peas and beans store nitrogen in nodules on their roots. This can be a real advantage to plants that occupy a growing space after them.

## offset
A side shoot that develops its own root system and can be separated from the parent plant to produce a new plant. Artichokes produce offsets.

## perennial
A plant that will live for many years, usually flowering each year. Many die back in the winter and reappear in the following spring.

## pinching out
Using the thumb and forefinger to remove, literally pinch out, the growth tips of a plant. Refers to side shoots of tomatoes or the growing tips of fava beans (broad beans).

## potassium
See NPK.

## resistant
Some plants have been shown or have been bred to have better resistance to pests and diseases; that is, they are less likely to be affected by an attack. Resistance, however, is not the same as complete immunity.

## runner
A thin stem produced by a mature plant on the end of which an immature plant will form, as with strawberry plants.

## set
When used of onions or shallots, "set" refers to the immature bulbs planted like seed. When used of flowers it means that the flower has been successfully fertilized and will produce a fruit.

## subsoil
The layer of soil under topsoil, usually infertile.

## taproot
A long tapered root, like that of a carrot or parsnip.

## thinning out
Removing some weaker seedlings to leave the remaining plants space to develop to maturity.

## transplants
Young plants that have been raised in one location or a pot and are moved to another. Plug plants are transplants.

## truss
A number of fruits, like tomatoes, growing down a single stem.

## true
When used about plants grown from seed, "true" means they will have the same characteristics as the parent plant. Plants raised from the seed of F1 hybrids will not be true.

## tuber
A bulbous, swollen stem or root that stores energy, like potatoes, Jerusalem artichokes, and dahlias.

# Index

# Acknowledgments

My special thanks go to Clive Nichols for his superlative photography and his endless patience and good humor. I am indebted to the publisher for the enthusiasm and faith shown in this project. My thanks to: Jason Douglas for his extraordinary hard work and uplifting sense of humor; Jon Hobson for great groundwork; and Peter Wheeler for his carpentry skills. To my parents for their support, listening to me enthuse about growing veg, and giving me some wonderful old tools. Finally heartfelt thanks go to my children, Harriet, Nancy, and Joshua, and husband, David, for their occasional help, willingly eating everything I grow (well almost), and indulging my passion for gardening.

Clare can be contacted via www.clarematthews.com

# Photo Credits

All photos are by Clive Nichols unless otherwise noted. The photograph on page 56 is by neil langan/ Shutterstock.